WOKELESS DICTIONARY
(A Wicked Wordbook)

Wokeless Dictionary (A Wicked Wordbook)

Steve Morgan

Published by Steve Morgan, 2023.

Also by Steve Morgan

A Standard Religiously Irrelevant Version (S.R.I.V) Twist of Fate
Edition
Wokeless Dictionary (A Wicked Wordbook)
DECONSTRUCTING ENDTIME DELUSIONS (A STUDY OF
CHRISTIAN ENDTIMES)

Table of Contents

WOKELESS DICTIONARY

(A Wicked Wordbook)

You're an idiot.
But you're *my* idiot.

LUV GOD.

ISBN: 9780645910520 (ebk)
ISBN: 9780645910537 (pbk)
Cover Image and design made using Canvar free.
www.canvar.com.au[1]

Typeset and design by draft2digital
Published with assistance of draft2digital
www.draft2digital.com[2]

A catalogue record for this title is available
from the National Library of Australia.

---

1.   http://www.canvar.com.au

2.   http://www.draft2digital.com

Copyright:

ACKNOWLEDGEMENT and DISCLAIMER:

Just if you are disturbed that this acknowledgement and disclaimer is complete flummery as any other. Countless personalities have used their skills, and expertise. I am just the plebeian who has utilised what has been offered, and with my imagination produced this work.

If you decide to be a reader of this dictionary, Thank-you. Without any of you taking the slightest interest. It would be a pointless exercise to compose this sarcastic, polemical wordbook of English words, and phrases. If wondering, this dictionary is not devoted to a god, parent, or significant other. This work is dedicated to world 'nobody's'. Those who for one reason or another, never seem to crack a mention in anything published. Such as, the trees, the engineers, and the countless other professionals; of education, sciences, book publishing, and the manufacturers of pulp; without any of these specialised fields it would not have been possible to have this work printed, in either hard book form, or electronic format.

Despite the mentioning of several religious and politically charged words, phrases. Entries of this silly dictionary were written as neutrally as possible, and were penned to lard those topics as they deserve. Using innuendo and rhetorical expression. Any adverse reaction that may arise while reading some sensitive topics of this book, is the inquietude of the reader alone. The author takes no responsibility for how an audience interprets the narrative. All were composed with a clear conscious. Devoid of malice. Distress is only your estimated understanding. At any point, you have always the ability to revoke all distressing moments. "Just as sure as all will 'face our own wall' one day, changing, or revising opinions are part of life. If you have not done this in a while, please have your pulse checked, - you may have expired already." (Adapted from the author's 'Standard Religiously Irrelevant Version' (S.R.I.V.). A bible of punned religious narratives). Cover designed using Canva free. www.canva.com.au[3]

SIGNS and SYMBOLS:

Adj. adjective.

  Acron. Acronym.

  N. Noun.

  v. Verb.

  est. Established.

  I.e. that is.

  Esp. especially.

  Abbr. abbreviation.

  Alt. Alternative.

  Obs. Obsolete. Often found at www.lexicophilia.com[4]

  Neo. Neologism. A newly coined, or reinvented explanation/ spelling to a standard word.

  Auth orig neo. Author's original neologism. As far as known these have not existed previously.

  c. Century. (16c = Sixteenth Century).

  Lat. latin.

  Gk. Greek.

  OE. Olde English - Bristow.

  OWT. Olde Worlde trade, occupation - Waters.

  ODUE. Official Dictionary of Unofficial English - Barrett.

  Lit. Literal.

  Suff. Suffix.

  Vulg. Of the vulgar tongue. Olde worlde language, descriptions.

AUTHOR'S FOREFACE:

Wehrds (words) are an amazing tool of civilisation. Nobody can escape them. Words, began a simple life, as mere wedge-shaped marks, and scratches, indentations on wet clay tablets. As triangles, lines, dots, dashes, scribbles, pictograms and the like. Then, we broadened our concepts. Noticing we could more effectively communicate in words which were much better, and more cognisable to others than body language. More effective and understandable than the former scratches, pits, indiscriminate marks, or those silly languages comprising squarks, screeches, growls, purr's, toots... invented by other varieties of animal. We had lost the ability to clearly communicate with beings unlike ourselves.

Many people think about words; how we stumbled upon speech, how we became proficiently utilisers of words. How words, can and affect lives. There are those who obsess over how many of these marks called words change, and shape a hominid life. Such an obsession has also occupied some nowadays whose ideas and uses of words are not so noble. Being an obsession to wield a variety of words in a manner similar to the growth of mould; as a cancerous backlash directed to someone opposed to the latest view. Not face to face however. For, that would expose an awful truth of those labelled the woke keyboard warriors. That these rabble rousers are not at all skilled words users. Rather, are more satiated and content in reliance on acronym, and emoji as their preferred Promethean Ninja to dispel the opponent. We also occupy ourselves with entertainment in words. When in the company of other people. We stole their expressions, and use of phrases, and idioms. Lots of us act out and change our objectives at the request of words. Our lives are enveloped in these strange markings, called letters that are strung together to form words. Some words excite and animate. Some words are intoxicating; inebriate, bumpsy, groggy, tired and emotional. While yet, others do have a tendency to become what they are; like boredom, one of the most boring invented. Or 'pathetic' the most pathetic we have devised. Or, 'dumb' the most intellectually challenging for inadvertently, *um* does interrupt the flow of speech. Causing us to forsake, and forget 'B'. Many words cause intrigues, enrage, and discourage. There are people who have a delight for words, and are skilled in their use. Others, are skilled in the misuse, such as um, "there use of words to make they're point is questionible. And, they do, misuse the rules of words. Like, starting sentences with, and..."

Using words causes more words to be employed. So it goes, on, and on. With the popularity of language, and expression using words, we decided we needed another device that would assist us in remembering what the hell we were talking about. Realising the grey matter between our jug handles was often inefficient, and ineffective as a complete storage unit. Voila! Another word was invented - dictionary. Here, we found that we could store a great stack of words for a variety of, and later use. Even when we didn't really understand what some of them meant. We even found we could occupy ourselves with silliness. Inventing, and manipulating words, and their meanings. Mocking how some looked, or were spelled.

This is a dictionary of fatuous, desipient daffynitions. An 'A' to Zed of paronomasia. Another of the many wordbooks that tell stories or drive the imagination through word play; another wordbook in likeness to those authored of an earlier dictionary full of quips, wisecracks, and some oddities of English words. Like those, and the earlier editions, this little dictionary too offers an array of mischievous quips in definitions to the entries to many ordinary, modern, and commonly used words, and phrases. Daffynitions to these, and many other words:

ACONITE: *The most opportune period a con-artist, or other criminal advantages in applying their trade.*

MASH POTATO: *Excreta deposited by a frightened ghost.*

WOKELESS DICTIONARY

SEVERAL: *To dismember everything.*

NEW TESTAMENT: *Old myths retold to suit abetter era.*

UNDERCLUB: *An underdeveloped <u>clubbable</u>*, and more.

In essence, this dictionary is an act of sarcastic wickedness. A punishing 'wokeless' wordbook displaying for enjoyment the wickedness to words, and modern phrases. Most entries comprise common words, and phrases. Those that could be found in standard dictionaries, or are in common use. The twist; the explanations offered to these words will either delight, or disgust. This is the beauty of English words; for within many can be noticed other words. It is the compound nature, and openness to imagination that allows a mischievous wordbook like this to be written. It is therefore anticipated that the entries in the coming pages are devilishly luciferin (illuminating). That they are ludic, and waggish for an audience. That readers are delighted to gambol through the entries. <u>Underline</u> words in an explanation/ definition, daffynition have their own silly entry.

Now this is not the end. It is not even the beginning of the end.

But it is, perhaps, the end of the beginning.

Winston Churchill

Enjoy!

STEVE MORGAN

"Fragile", and "Handle with Care" have always been interpreted by postal employees as, "Launch with accuracy".
Author, a former postal employee.

Logolepsy (logo-lepsi)
-seize, embrace, have fun with words.

Calories

(noun)

Tiny creatures that live in your closet and sew your clothes a little bit tighter every night.

A:

A: (ay, a)

• Colloquial Australian greeting.

• Abbr. form hey, or hi. "Ay, how the bloody hell are ya?"

• The alphabetical letter some people were forced to wear as a mark of disgrace. Esp., if found to have dabbled in, or accused of adultery.

• Almost exclusive employment as a prefix, or indefinite article.

• 'A' is considered a word in itself.

• Top class, best standard.

• Often begins sentences.

• The first letter of the alphabet.

• Denotes random items.

• 'A' = 'activist'. The extremist zealot who is more interested in misinformation, propaganda, indoctrination than reality, reason, and logic.

AB:

• (Lat) Prefix, against, from, away.

• n. Human blood type.

- Eleventh month of the Jewish civil, and 5th month religious calendar. Usually, coinciding with July, August of modern calendars.

- Abbr. antibody, biology.

- Abbr. abdominal.

- In the Egyptian *Book of the Dead*, AB, in symbolic form is a heart being weighed. Representing the will, emotion, and passions.

ABASEMENT:

The <u>keep</u> where disgraceful, humiliating, contemptuous or embarrassing clutter that should always be hidden, and safely stored.

ABACK:

The spinal column housing.

ABACTION: (OE)

The secret auction of bovine herds.

AIR SUPPLY:

- Aust. Pop group, est., 1975.

- (ODUE) shoddy workmanship. When tasks are paid for but incomplete, or nonexistent.

- Much more life enhancing than becoming <u>breathless</u>.

ABED:

Where rest is attained.

ABET:

A gambler's attraction.

ABUT:

Your posterior, hind, rear end.

ABLUSH:

The cause, and outcome of embarrassment.

ABIT:

See, bit.

ABOMINATION:

Those loathsome, detestable nations who persevere in a rejection that human life is polytheistic by nature.

ACARPOUS:

Feline happy to recline on the parcel shelving of the back seat of a vehicle.

ACCLAIM:

Insurance paperwork.

ACCOMPLICE:

Takes more than a single wingless parasite to be classified pediculosis.

ACCORD:

- Flexible string of twisted strands.
- A power delivery system for electronic appliances.

ADAMITE:

The original minute arachnid skin infestation inhabiting all life.

ADAM:

- Earthy name of the believed progenitor to humankind.
- A reservoir constructed to retain water.

ADONIS:

- Mafia term of endearment for the don of the family, and business.
- Babylonian myth: a term applied to the deity Tammuz.

ABADDON:

A destructive, misguided, untrustworthy adonis.

ABBOT:

Artificial Intelligent (A.I.) monk.

AIRBAG:

A flatulent parodic performer.

AIRFORCE:

A measurement of expelled windiness.

ANASTROPHE:

You a put when inverse sentences in wrong the order.

ABBA:

Swedish patriarch who formed a rock group.

APPOINTED TO SUMARIA: (Auth orig neo)

<u>Death</u>, died.

AERO:

- Chocolate.
- Manufacturer of the most precise lawn bowl.

ABBREVIATE:

- A snak.
- Fast food.

AFIX:

Done deal.

AFAR:

Very distant from the current position.

AFFUSE:

A safety device for electrical appliances.

AFIELD:

Wide open spaces for leisure.

AFLAME:

Flickering bush telly.

AGIST:

Understanding the general sense.

ABATIS: (ah-bat-is)

- Nocturnal flighted mammal.

- A fortification.

- Sporting equipment used to swat a projectile thrown in your direction, in hopes to score a home run.

- A wooden implement with a handle used to defend three sticks from a projectile turfed at them. To miss the projectile is to be unceremoniously told to depart a field of play, with jibing from opponents, after being given the 'finger'.

ADVERSARY:

University for the antagonist. Remember to always <u>advice</u> to the mind upon <u>arrival</u> at classes.

ALIGHT:

A manufactured agent that illuminates darkened regions.

ALPHABET:

The original time a wager was placed, which set in motion the addiction of a gambler.

ARK/ARC:

- The ligneous bathtub that Noah (bible) was directed to fashion, and fabricate. Despite a lack in any neptunist skills, being someone unlikely to have witnessed any torrential water courses in his 600year lifespan Noah was approved. The tub was to safe-keep <u>pears</u>, and several immediate family members, and a couple of animal breeders; either one <u>pair</u>, or two are unknown for sure. That is, it was to house 1.5million species. Which included the 400 or so that were violent tward humankind? Noah was instructed; thus, because a deity had decided to deracinate with omnicide; that a liquidation of all Humankind's, and eve's, and all creations should be visited upon them. All but the residence of the tub were dismembered from <u>life</u>, when the deity sent a maelstrom across a certain region. A cause of his losing the plot when he did realise he'd made a big creative boo boo when they refused to pay homage.

- A special cupboard that houses the Jewish sacred writings.

- A low unit complex set aside for the housing of livestock.

- The curved trajectory of a very high voltage. A cause of Thor disciplining a daydreaming junior deity with a whack on his table with his hammer.

AFTERLIFE:

- The thinly veiled concept believed by god-mythologists, stating: after taking formal residence with a wooden overcoat, a 'new' personal lifecycle of better standing than the one experience on Earth is not only possible, but a certainty.

- The disapproval that the catatonic state we will all experience is not really permanent, or an inescapable certainty.

- An immortality concept which gave rise to the 'us', and 'them' apartheid. 'Us' - the religionist is afforded the transportation of the discarnate soul of the expired into a much better abode of pure happiness. 'Them' - the rest, are condemned to a barbecue reception that can only be described as the dream-state of a sadist.

AGNOSTIC:

Anyone unaware of the totality that religious falsehoods are empirically verified, and documented. So, blissfully declare from ignorance, that although highly unlikely, it is not really possible to deduce with surety whether deities exist.

AMAZE:

Labyrinth of confusion.

AMBO:

Paramedic.

ARREST:

Cease movement to recuperate.

ANTE-MATTER:

The situation, conditions preceding the believed rapid expansion of significance, the Big Bang Moment. Which then birthed the theory of everything.

Question: which African heavyweight would make a great crime boss? Answer: AWRY-noseros.

ADVERSITIVE:

The degree earned by adversity students.

APROXIMATING:

Proxy dating site for amorous downloadable applications.

AUSSIENTAL: (Auth orig neo)

Australian citizens of mixed heritage.

AIRDROP:

That tiny <u>bit</u> of liquid expelled during <u>airforce</u> exercises caused you to <u>asperse</u>.

ABREAST:

• The non-sexist egalitarian term given to chest glands, mammaries of both male, and female apelike species.

• The delectable portion of <u>cackling cheat</u> meat.

• A woman's appendage of delight for many school boys, and gentlemen alike. Some call these waps, an 'Apple dumplin shop', comfort stations, or various other terms of endearment.

ALLOTMENT:

Effie - (Greek) Australian sitcom character vernacular (Acropolis Now). Means - very much, way more than <u>alittle</u>.

AIRSTRIP:

Skid-mark left in one's clothing after an <u>airdrop</u>!

ABNORMAL:

• Deviation from the accepted thought.

• (Modern) conservative, or other politician, public servant, <u>bureaucrat</u>, socialist <u>radical</u> who dare stray the party line. Displaying true principals, morals, ethical standards that are accepting of another's view without choking on the barbs of '<u>critical race theory</u>', or other nonsense.

AGATE:

Small hinged barrier allowing for a separation or acceptance of another side.

ARRIVAL:

A competitor, nemesis, contestant, challenger to your point of view.

ALITTLE:

Not as much as <u>allotment</u>. Even less than <u>allot</u>.

ALLOT:

More than <u>alittle</u>, but not as much as <u>allotment</u>.

ARCHDEACON:

Hunchback elderly ecclesiastical dignitary.

ADAMITE:

The primeval parasite.

ANTHEM:

Yet another personal pronoun of the confused.

ARRANT:

Notoriously snobbish, opinionated insect.

ABRIDGE:

Structure to traverse with more ease all manners of difficult terrain.

AMBROSPHYNX: (Auth orig neo - ambro-sfinks)

Compound: Ambrosia + Sphynx.

Ambrosia: the famed tonic of gods. Much likened to bee bread. Sphynx: the hairless North American feline. To save the embarrassment of this breed of feline in public Ambrosphynx is the tonic marketed to be used to reverse its balding. So pleasing is its tase and smell, it is likened to bee bread, and so is also a food stuff.

ANTELOPE:

- Opposite to <u>absquatulate</u>.
- Interchangeable with <u>cantaloupe</u>.

ABIGAIL:

A mighty, tempestuous wind.

ABRAM:

- Conventional method of transportation of toddlers, and newborns.

- (Metaphysical) - naked.

- The title given by a frightful personality of Bible fame, Terah to one of his sons. Maybe, in recognition that the child refused to use his <u>chevroshanks</u> until being forced to after Terah's death. Abram, would often revert to using an innovative rundle instead as it was much more comfortable, and much quicker. Meaning, play dates, and the like could be more enjoyable as nobody had to wait for extended periods for him to catch up.

AVERAGE:

• (OE) To fertilise land with manure, or seaweed.

• (Conventional) typically uninspired, unexceptional, humdrum, indifferent age.

ASENT:

• Adj. lacking attendance.
• n. Pleasant, or repellant odour.

ABACUS:

Well educated, calculated, and executed snipe tward someone, or thing. Typically directed from behind, or a hidden safety. Such as, the anonymity of a troll on social media.

ABUNDANCE:

• The hairstyle after effect, consequence at waking after a night out. Typically, following passing out. The following morning waking with a bad case of 'bed head'. Mostly an affliction of women. But, can be an affliction felt by any male sporting a man-bun.

• See calamistrate.

ADADAH:

- Line of a festive tune composed by musician Sting: Adadah, dah, dah; ado, do, do.

- In acknowledgment of a male parent.

ACCURSER:

A most unruly, foul-mouthed rowdy individual. Bent on using vulgarities, insults, slurs. Always, directed tward an opponent for the purposes of incrimination, or denouncement.

AFTERBIRTH:

- <u>Life</u> ensues.
- Precedes <u>death</u>.

ABDUCTION:

- Force used to restrict a migrating water fowl.
- A cynical way to describe a property foreclosure.
- (Symbolic) punishment, loss of control.

'ARSON':

Upperclass introduction of male progeny.

ABHORRENT:

The rent a round heal, grande horizontale is forced to pay their procurer.

ABETTER, ABETTOR:

Newer, superior way.

ABELISM:

Any speech, correspondence recalled or found in the archives that were left by the bible character <u>abel</u>.

ABEL: (neo)

Brother to Cane (bible). He was very much 'differently abel' to his brother. Who chose environmental concerns over the professions of <u>cower</u>, and barntender that abel chose.

ABSQUATULATE: (ab-skwat-u-late)

• To depart hurriedly.

• A brilliant <u>wehrd</u> to <u>discombobulate</u> a squatter you wish to remove from an unlawful occupation.

ABROGATE:

To rescind entry to a male only entrance.

ABEDNEGO:

Mate of <u>shadrach</u> (bible book Daniel).

AGOG:

The one half of a Jewish Temple refusing to accept that people are predisposed to <u>syn</u>.

ABMOSQUIOS: (Auth orig neo - ab-mos-kwi-os)

Having the blood type we each crave, repellant to sanguisugent bugs. From ab (lat) from, away + human blood type + mosquito + 'ous', nature of.

AMPHIBOLOGY:

Obscured inexactness.

ALTERNATIVE:

- An opposing ideology of another national entity.

- Opposing reality, historic fact.

- A goal of Transhumance.

- A goal of trans-humanism. Their scientific experimentation of seamless integration of machine, and human.

- Transformation of national pride from one state, to another.

ABACTOR:

Refusal of financial backing of a theatrical performer/ production.

ABASED:

Degraded headquarters for operations.

ABUTTER:

An agressive geep.

ASSVOGEL: (slang)

Jackassification.

ABNORMOUS:

Unusually large rodent.

ARTICIFER:

Lucifer's personal servant.

ABCEDARIAN:

Proficient in all genre's of literature.

ADAMANT:

Insect's first creation.

ADVERTI:

Illuminati of the adversity.

ABOVE-BORED: (neo)

Not quite stupefied.

ABNORMOUS SAPIEN:

(Horace) wise without knowledge.

ABRACADABRA:

Belief in a resurrection.

AMEN:

- Nonsensical plurality: man.

- Delusional exclamation, and affirmation of god-mythologists that something completely unknown is a fact.

ABSENTEE:

To your room without dinner for misbehaving.

ACCOST:

Prices paid before bartering.

AFTERWARD:

Hospital waiting room for discharged patients.

ADHERE:

No deviation.

ADULT:

To move, change from last month. To purposefully doctor (falsify) reports of previous month. 'Ult', from Ultimo - 'of last month'.

AMUN: (ahr-moon)

- Paramount deity worshipped in ancient Egypt. Equated with the sun deity Ra.

- The orb of dulled brightness witnessed in night skies.

ADVICE:

To increase, escalate, expand, strengthen wicked, immoral behaviour.

AGENDA:

Common practice of modernity. A wish to reverse, or disassociate oneself from a birth genda. Insisting that all others comply, and acknowledge on pains of cancellation, chosen pronoun designations or other nonsenses. There are a variety of 'genda's' these days. Which are spoken of:

- Biological genda.
- Grammatical genda.
- Legal genda.
- Self-identified genda.
- Perceived genda.
- Experienced genda. (See 'Gender' - "Key Words for Today".)

AFFINITY:

What happened to the empathy for what may arise after infinity? Is infinity truly boundless? How will any of us know?

AIRLING:

Defying gravity.

ANTIC:

Infant insect.

AFFLUENT SOCIETY:

A society most susceptible to the erupting devastations of an influenza epidemic.

ACUMEN:

Queue of blokes.

ANGUILLA:

Angry, guerrilla freedom fighter.

AUF:

- (OWT) simpleton, halfwit, dunce.

- Mythology: manifestation of Egypt's deity Ra. Specifically as the dead Ra traversing the night skies.

AFFLATUS:

- An aerating device, or instrument.

- Some other that gave nascent imagination, intuition, and creativity. Before the enlightenment, this was a deity, or those considered instruments of the deity; known by the ancients as 'Oracles'. With the advancement of science all people can become like an 'oracle'. Harnessed through meditation, and brainwave synchronicity by meditative brainwave entrainment.

ACCRUE:

A band of misfits used to deceive people of their earnings in ever greater quantities.

ABITER: (ahr-by-tur)

The increased pain, or annoyance of anything that punctures, pricks, or gnaws.

AVARICIOUS: (av-uh-RISH-is)

A bird that steals items from another to better their own standing, and prospects of finding a partner whose eyes are focussed on bling, and other pretty things.

AUGUR: (aw-ger)

Roman predictions of words becoming common.

ASQUE:

Queue of asses.

ALMERY:

Storage unit of spare prosthetic arms, limbs, and other parts.

ACCUBATION: n. (ak-u-bay-shon)

Bad mannered young carnivore who would rather laze about the couch than assist with family meal preparation, capture.

ANGER:

- (Christian mythology) deadly syn.
- (Reality) an emotionally justified reaction to an injustice.

ARISTOTLE:

Earliest Gk. philosopher of reason who understood, and taught that self-evident laws of nature need not be attributed to a metaphysical entity. That each could be sufficiently grasped through logical reasoning. Dante, attributing him as "a master of all who know."

ALLITTERATE:

Fully versed, enlightened Aristotelian society.

ACEBRITY:

Highly praised theatrical performer.

ACONITE:

The most opportune period a con-artist, or other criminal advantages in applying their trade.

ACOUSTIK: (ahr-kow-stik)

- Cattle prod.

- Annoying properties, quality of sounds rather not heard through walls in hotels.

ACROMATICAL:

Dancing while under an influence which leads to noticing the pretty shapes, and colours of the surrounds.

ACRITA:

Insect.

ACROSTIK: (Auth orig neo - ak-ross-tik)

Similar to an acoustik, in that it is a device of discipline. Used by educators, and other authority personalities. Accepted prior to the world becoming a 'snowflake', soft-headed, and perpetually upset; unable or willing to accept any form of reprimand, scolding, rebuke regardless of applicability, and appropriateness.

ADAGE:

- Prefix.
- Advantage.
- Advertisement.
- Anno domini - the age of now.

AWHAPER: (neo - ahr-wapur)

Real big ferfie, lie, invention.

AUSTRALIESE: (neo)

Colloquial Australian tongue.

AUSPICE: (Auth orig neo)

- (Pop group) Australian member - 'Spice girls'.
- Aussie bush foods, spices, condiments.

AVOIDER:

Vague of mind.

A.I.: (Artificial Intelligence)

Mechanical abilities to carry out the functions of human intelligence and menial tasks. Is more than mere 'smart' technologies - robotic, computer intelligence. Specified in the field as 'machine intelligence'. Differentiating it from malevolent Sci-fi depictions of murderous intelligent machines. Includes the technologies framed around:

- Voice detection.
- Facial detection.
- Crowd counting and monitoring software.
- Skeletal detection.
- Vital organ recognition, targeting.
- Human bio-field detection.
- Emotional detection, analysis.

All which are currently being developed, enhanced, and utilised by State authorities, and private tech companies for the manipulation, coercion, control of populations. That they might usher in a desired utopia, system of authoritative governance. Many are unaware for these technologies are announced using the propaganda of 'need, safety, security, and over all beneficial' requirement of a healthy, stable society. Pity the mores of those captured.

AVOIDLESS:

Very astute.

AVOIDANCE:

Being the dance routine of an <u>avoider</u> while influenced by multiple mind-altering substances.

ACANTHOUS;

The unpleasantness of 'pins 'n needles'.

ASSISTANCE:

The Eve of insect creation.

ACCOUPLE: (obs)

Joint venture.

ADIPOSE: ('adee-pose)

Opposite to raw-of-bone, non fatty.

ARMS-END:

- Your hands.
- (Extreme) fingers.

APHRODIZIAC: (Auth orig neo)

Boofy hairstyle causing a fluctuating spin.

APPLE:

- <u>Arrival</u> to Microsoft.

- Variety of crisp, round crunchy fruit of various colours, textures. Often used in pies.

- Bad as...

- Rotten...

- To compare ... and pears.

- The Operating system used to compose this dictionary.

- One a day is said to keep a saw-bone away.

ANZAC:

Biscuit celebrating the alliance of the Australian and New Zealand culinary achievements during periods of conflict.

ANYTHING:

<u>Bit</u> of a silly personal pronoun that someone, somewhere is bound to attach to themselves out of desperation of a specialised, but nonsensical recognition.

ACERSERCOMIC: (uh-kar-sue-kah-mik)

Sampson. Before his unfortunate encounter with the malicious, cunning, hairdresser Delilah, (Bible:- Judg 16:17).

ACHLOROPSIA: (uh-klor-opsee-uh)

Never envious, jealous.

ABSURD:

Opinions that are seen as erratic, and so are acting at variance to one's own.

ASPERSE:

When your body sends another a kiss. Commonly called a fart.

AGE-OTORI: (aah-gey-toh-ree)

(Japanese) the feeling, exclamation voiced after attending a hairdresser employed by Delilah. Noticing the rearrangement of your style into an abundance.

ACEDIA: (uh-ce-dia)

A modern disease. Frankly, I just have no care for.

ARHWRONGNIUM: (Auth orig neo - uh-rong-ne-um)

[inspired from article by Salvatore Babones 'Wrongnium' - Quadrant Online]

Little-known element of journalism. A Journalist's code. Extensively used by modern media in pushing fake news of misinformation, disinformation where a biased, one-sided argument devoid of reason, logic, or empirical evidence is espoused.

AWEFULIZE/ AWFULIZE: (Auth orig neo/

ODUE)

- Fully awe inspired.
- Fully expecting failure, or a dreadful outcome.

B:

B: (bee)

• A winged insect much different to a fly. Not as near annoying. Much more helpful, and productive. Assisting with pollination of plant life. Also, the producer of a great yellowish substance, sweet and sticky, derived from nectar, and pollen. Enjoyed by humans on toast and other foodstuffs, and other creatures. Like relatives of Yogi bear, and Whinny the Poo. Lives in a metropolis, or, as a loner when banned from social activities by the monarch for displaying too often irritation of others' company. So, did spike them with his javelot/barb. Causing hurt feelings, and sometimes causing the distressful effects of anaphylaxis.

• B's knees.

• Standard of grading. Not quite as good as 'A'.

• Lower-graded entertainment. Such as a <u>corn</u> production.

• The Hebrew alphabet (B) represents a house. A 'But and Ben' - Two room dwelling. BUT = kitchen, inner room. BEN, outer room.

• B - likely signified the forehead branding of <u>Cane</u> by the deity. Just as 'A' was the official branding for some, so too 'B'. Used to signify the blasphemer, <u>cynic</u> who dared question, or speak ill of a deity.

• One-eyed hunchback.

• Collective meeting for leisure, or work.

BEQUEST:

A crusade, adventure of bee armies in efforts to secure, reclaim provinces for their latest buzz religion.

BUM NUT:

Egg.

BEESTING:

Delightful glazed cake filled with whipped cream/honey.

BETWEENITY:

Median state intervening young person, and adult.

BREATH BURNER: (Auth orig neo)

An incessant jabberer.

BIPOLAR:

• Reversible waistcoat.

• Moody bear. Depressed one moment for lack of honey. Then, hyperactive at stealing some.

BRIDGEABLE:

To remain relatable, different communities must concede their bias against building bridges to strengthen relations.

BARRACKS:

Where pool cues are stored at pubs.

BARRAGE:

The causes of pub fights.

BARROW:

Not quite a <u>barrage</u>.

BARRISTER:

Publican.

BARMASTER:

Interchangeable with <u>barrister</u>.

BARMOTE: (OE)

Dusty pub countertop.

BEDLAM WORKER: (OE)

Staff member of the confused; Charge nurse of inmates/ residence of a madhouse (asylum).

BARRING:

Enclosure surrounding combatants at bar fights. Spectators forming a ring about them. Much like children do at school.

BECAME:

Was, but is no more.

BECOME:

Is, and will be.

BELONG:

Stretched.

BACCHUS:

Ancient festival celebrating extreme drunkenness.

BIRTH-CONTROL GLASSES: (ODUE)

See coke-bottle.

BESIDE:

Not in front, or behind, underneath, or above. But, on level pegging.

BENJAMINE:

Ancient ancestor to all DJ's, musician, and music producers.

BENJAMINITE:

- Work experience benjamine.
- Parasite that causes the affliction of an earworm.

BARRATEEN:

To prohibit social, and sporting activities, participation of an unruly teen as punishment for misbehaviour.

BILLHOUSE: (OE)

- Bank.
- Constabulary headquarters (U.K.).

BALDRIC:

The dull minded character, and offsider to blackadder.

BEFOREHAND:

Your arm.

BABBALOG:

- Official name given to the musical talents of a Babylonian Olde Worlde songbird - babbler.

- Official incoherent notes, records scribbled by a resident of the (bible) township of Babel attempting to explain how their fortitude failed dramatically.

- Wedge-shaped pits, marks, indentations of a Cuneiform Tablet. Earliest known form of script/writing developed in the Middle East; Ancient Sumeria. It spread throughout Mesopotamia. Being used extensively throughout the Ancient Middle Eastern regions as the official political communication.

BELITTLE:

Slightly larger than a pigmy.

BOGOF: (acron - buy 1, get 1 free)

Wasting hard earned money in the purchase of an item, gadget that will likely become obsolete within the year after purchase. Considering: the purchase likely cost more than manufacturing, so in reality the consumer secured the second item free. The difference, the manufacturer knows of their deceit. So, the second item is often labelled 'free'.

BLANQUIT:

- (OE) Course blanket.
- Caribbean songbird, a Quit, with limited song repertoire.

BIGAMY: (Fat Amy)

(Movie character) Pitch Perfect character, played by Rebel Wilson.

BADITUDES: (Auth orig neo)

Ten commands/ instructions for troublemakers.

BOBBIN:

Act of floating in water.

BORING:

Sister city to dull (Scotland).

BOOBY TRAP:

- Brassiere worn by women.
- Set an ambush for a stupid person.

BRIEFCASE:

Not a <u>longcase</u>.

BROKEN:

Concerning the extent of knowledge, and understanding had about one's brother.

BLACK HOLES:

- Undetectable existence in space. Escaping illumination, and empirical evidence.

- An ever expanding ⊙.

- Never forget a torch. It will become very handy when searching the depths of space for these anomalies. Simply for the disappearance of that light when found, [black holes consume everything in their grasp. Light cannot escape its grip].

- A term explaining organisations, and interested parties whose sole purpose is the propagation, and dissemination of <u>disinformation</u> to the widest population demographic possible. Particularly, clandestinely with sprinklings of truth to instil believability. For control, manipulation, coercion of people through <u>fear</u>. Example: the push by government to increase their authoritarian power-grab over citizens, through disinformation, and <u>misinformation</u> legislature; that societies required a lockdown to 'save lives', as a Covid-19 Pandemic response. Both are mistruths proving that through such draconian measures, governments do not trust their citizens.

BOGGART: (bo-gart - OE)

[Humphrey] - a famous American theatrical performer. Starring now as a spectre.

BERGMASTER: (OE)

Highly skilled, efficient fast-food employee, consumer.

BLOODLETTER:

- Ransom note.
- Saw-bone, medical professional.

BLU-DEVIL:

An imp cast from the guild for displaying empathy for victims.

BOILER MAKER:

Anyone that makes another furious.

BARKING HOUSE:

Kennel.

BALDERDASH:

Athletics event for the hairless, balding athlete.

BALUSTER:

An amorous <u>geep</u>.

BARCODE:

The official code of conduct expected in bars, clubs, pubs, and other public venues. The explicit outlined rules of engagement, service, procedures that govern both publican, and patron.

BANANA-SPLIT:

An evasive, unpredictable divorce procedure.

BAROMETER:

- Device to check the alcoholic content of beverages.

- Electronic means of assessing, and enforcing the <u>barcode</u>. Esp., after noticing they have acquired a substantial elephants trunk, have become 'tired, and emotional'.

BAG-DRAG: (OE)

Careworn, fatigued, knackered elderly impersonator still applying the trade.

BIANRY: (Auth orig neo)

Confused canary.

BONK: n.

• The annoying sound indicating a computer key function is unavailable, and so cannot be performed.

• The state of being exhausted. No longer able to participate.

• (Slang) euphemism of carnality.

BAMBOO:

Ghostly, frightening apparition, noise of a deceased geep.

BLANDISHMENTS:

Unappealing crockery.

BOOSE/BOWSE: (OE)

Tavern, roadhouse, alehouse, bar, club of relaxation of cattle, drovers, and their dogs after a long day in the field.

BASOPHOBIA:

Disease of the mind. A vexing condition particularly after breakage of bones that would fair much better in their original condition. Fear of falling. Fortunately, many people are immune, choosing to remain firmly planted to terra firma. So, are disaffected by such phantasms. This condition is often accompanied by acrophobia - fear of heights. Best to steer clear of ladders, or jumping recklessly over jagged rocks, or traversing slippery surfaces if diagnosed with either affliction. Base-jumping, and like activities like free fall are unquestionably silly. Such activities surely ensures both torments are serviced simultaneously.

BIGOTRY:

The conceited unrestrained try-hard wanna be.

BULLWACKER:

Defeating nonsense with intelligence, and giftedness in words.

BUTTERSCOTCH:

Scottish <u>abutter</u>.

BUREAUCRACY:

The strange powerful mad elite class who have a penchant for proving their ignorance, and insanity by enforcing the wider population to comply to their ideologically driven agenda.

BENIGN:

One hour after eight.

BAWBLING:

- Passionless ranting.
- Dull, pointless jewellery.

BAAJET: (Auth orig neo)

Ruminant Airliner. More cost effective than other standard ruminant cargo transports. Having only standing room for those named Shawn; saving on weight distribution.

BAM-PUDDLER: (Auth orig neo)

Introduced to the world stage in the Cambrian age by a neoteric Neanderthal. Daughter of the Croods, she invented a new entertainment system. A device to play with while other family members busied themselves; mulling about their bush tellies, or, attempting to train for domestic duties, <u>fire</u>. So successful was this gadget, it was soon commissioned as a multi-task labor-saving invention with wide applications. Not only could it occupy the youngest of any brood, being their play companion. But, was also employed by other members as the device of choice for tenderising meats, and other foodstuffs. Was also at a later period employed as a security measure. Being a much safer device for transport, when relocation, or an eviction notice arrived at the antre. It was much less destructive than previous 'fire' alarm systems; the bam-puddler could be moved without causing crispiness to its handler. Unlike fire who was often snarky at being moved, and often required to be totally reset/ reenergised. The bam-puddler too, was much easier to maintain, and happy to be left alone for extended times. Despite the odd occasion, it was stolen by a predator.

It neither required constant and laborious feeding, and attention; unlike fire who required both. Most of all, the bam-puddler was contented to remain at, or near the entrance of a dwelling, being pre-primed, never requiring batteries, it never ventured out on its own unlike fire when the weather turned inclement; cold, hungry, wet. The true value of the bam-puddler however, was realised at its effectiveness at dispelling intruders, or any undesirable intrusion. Crood family members suddenly began whacking relentlessly, whatever frightened, or startled them. The raucous alerting others to attend the party. Where much sore heads and other extremities followed.

Much time had lapsed, and after countless occupational changes; it was decided that the bam-puddler required occupational therapy. It was decided soon after to file for a name change, receiving the official, and more prestigious, and marketable title - <u>clubbable</u>.

BULLDOZER:

Pernicious, boring politician.

BRAINWASHING:

(An occurrence from birth). The inception, and infiltration of certain beliefs by deception, and stealth. Particularly, of the dogmatic god-mythologist, and political persuader or, the environmentalist enthusiast/numbskull.

BEAST:

Kind of easterly direction: over there, somewhere there, to the right of your position (when facing Northerly).

BROWNIST: (OE)

Earliest sect of <u>puritan</u>.

BOOTCATCHER: (OE)

A concierge who catches boots of hotel patrons.

BEGGAR BANGER: (OWT)

Official thug employed to remove vagrants, misfits, loiterers, beggars, and other undesirables from the street.

BEMIRE:

- Mud camouflage of foot soldiers.
- Beauty mudpack.

BACON:

Wolf in geep disguise.

BRUSHING THE ROAD: (OE)

Pothole repair.

BOTTOMING TOOL: (OE)

Medical device of rectal exploration/examination.

BOTTOM FEEDER: (Auth orig neo)

The 'ordinary' citizen. As the environmentalist, globalist, politically correct politicians designate other classes of society. That they are restricted, or banned from consuming, or purchasing food varieties that are deemed by these 'elite classes' as reprehensible, or out right damaging to society. For example, fast foods, containing high salt, fat content.

BOY BISHOP: (OE)

Underaged drunkard. [Bishop] a distilled alcoholic beverage.

BIOSPHERE:

Magical chainstore outlet that sells all manners of spherical objects. Hard, soft, bouncy, fat, skinny, large, small, flatter.

BOON-DOCKING:

To live as a Neanderthal. Chancing the poker by forsaking the security offered by owning the latest <u>clubbable</u>.

BRIEFING:

Not a <u>longing</u>.

BULL:

- Papal edict.
- Expletive exclamation.
- Cattle patriarch.

BIFACIAL:

- A hypocrite speaking opposing; simultaneous gabble - from both sides of their mouth.

- A politician, world leader.

- See <u>bothsideness</u>.

BOOTCAMP:

Disciplinary restraint of lower limbs.

BUMPTOUS:

- Anything in reach of a <u>clubbable</u>.
- The toffee nosed.
- Corrugated <u>road</u>, path.

BLACKADDER:

• Comedic British sitcom history. Told through the antics of Rowan Atkinson, and Ben Elton. Famous for its persistent confabulations, and punishments.

• (Vulgar) tanned accountant.

BREASTAURANT:

(Bit risqué) Breastfeeding.

BROBDINGNAGAIN:

A frabjously great word. Much greater than sizeable, bunyanesque, enormous, immense, vast, large, pythonic, mammoth, pantagruelian, biggest, big, giant, or gigantic, or even humongous. All these are but a pin-prick, and dwarfish in comparison.

BUDGET-DUST (Fluff):

• The rarest commodity of the average punter.
• Surplus finances of the well-to-do.

BACKWEHRDS: (neo)

• More interesting than the dullness of 'end word.'

• An afterwehrd.

• Parts of a story, or piece of literature that is at the furthermost part from the beginning of a text.

• An articulated rebuke.

BIT:

What is this all about? A 'bit' of what? Where did this bit come from? Does anyone truely know what a bit is? Is it a 'somewhat', a 'short distance'? Is 'quite large' a bit? The best practices of this bit thing seem to be suffering multiple personalities, so possibly is redundant to expression. Besides who determined that bit had to be anything? If 'bit' is <u>anything</u> who gave it the permission to invade, and ruin life, and everything else. By persisting the pronoun anything had to be a 'bit'!

TO Be, OR NOT TO Be. (Where, and why is it anyway?):

A <u>bit</u> of a philosophical conundrum. Particularly for:

- Students preparing for an exam, or lecture.

- Grey-lead pencil artists. What shading is best for their work?

- Why is this a question? Was 'Deep Thought' (Hitchhiker's Guide to the Galaxy) who was asked to calculate the answer of: The Universe, Life, and Everything. Concluding it had to be - 42! Which, undeniably is more profound than a silly question about whether or not to be.

- Do not think to be, just do!

BIBLE:

- Simply means, book.

- An antiquated book revered by god-mythologists for its fancies. Unknown by many is that several titles of the earliest printed texts of this book leave much to be desired. For instance:

• A (1551) edition was titled: "The Bug Bible". The title derived from a translation of one Hebrew word found in Psalm 95:5, as 'the terror'. Which was translated in the 16th century, as Bug. The oldest meaning being an object of fear. Thus, titled the Bug Bible. Might this then be reinterpreted to become "The Nightmare Version"?

• "The Treacle Bible" - (1549). Possibly the "sweetest, and stickiest" Version compiled yet.

• "The Wicked Bible" - (1632). Possibly, an early edition of the Devil's Bible, or most likely, the "Adultery Version". As passages condemning adultery were deleted during printing.

• "The Vinegar Bible" - (1717). A version to be read on fish, and chip nights.

• "The Idol Bible" - (1809). Clearly, not a best seller. Rather sitting around and barely read, except by those who were indolent themselves.

BLISTURD:

Alleviation after 'covering your feet'. ('Covering feet'. A Jewish euphemism for toileting. Comes from a passage in 1 Sam 24:3 where it is read that Saul (unknowingly) entered the very cave where David was hiding, to relieve himself.)

BIDENTAL:

Mutton.

BLANDISH:

- Unappealing meal.
- Somewhat insipid.

BLOAT:

Overcrowded vessel.

BUTTERFLY:

An insect attracted to the dag of <u>abutter</u>.

BACHELOR'S BUTTON:

- Bellybutton of a single male.
- (Vulg) male toggle, phallus.

BREAKAGE:

Time lapses between birthdays.

BONUS:

- Pay rise for executives, or any other who manages to successfully hustle the poor into accepting what they do not need, while fleecing them of what they do necessary.

- Congratulations to a treasurer: Best practice award for diddling the ledger, to swindle the governed population.

BOOMERANG:

Confrontational phone call from an <u>x</u> before settlement.

BRATWURST:

Godawful butter print, urchin sausage.

BAKING:

Royalty geep.

BAT: (Vulg)

Street worker, lady of the night.

BUMBLING:

- Buttock bling.
- Gaudy, unappealing jewellery.

BOIANT: (buoyant - neo)

Adam's first pet.

BOTTLER:

Adept at self-intoxicating.

BOOTLESS:

Naked feet.

BLOCKADE AUSTRALIA:

(Activists) destructive sanctimonious, petulant whiners demanding that their namesake be changed to "Blockhead Australia".

BOUNCER:

- <u>Biosphere</u>.
- Nightclub/ pub ruffian.

BUSHRANGER:

Electrical equipment sophisticated enough to take measurements that determine latitude, span, and/ or limit of a wilderness.

BOW: (bou)

Bark, minus any wow!

BEETLE CRUSHERS:

Footware.

BREATHLESS:

Deceased.

BUCCANEER: (OE)

Rodeo rider/ performer.

BOANERGES: (bo-aner-gees - OWT)

Preacher of doom.

BURNISH:

Barely singed, scorched, blackened.

BUCKALOOSE: (ODUE)

An unhinged, crazy uncontrolled <u>buccaneer</u> - out to lunch!

BUSKIN:

- S.U.V..
- Minibus.

BOTHSIDEDNESS/ BOTHSIDENESS:

The magical ability of politicians, charlatans, world leaders to argue a point from both ends of the mouth, at the same time; one side a positive idiosyncrasy, then, from the other enforcing a negative. The two often meet in the middle as a confused, indecipherable incoherence. Simply called - gobbledegook.

BOOT PARTYING:

Smashing, or treading heavily upon someone, or something in a fit of rage.

BONE BOX:

- (Vulg) mouth, as in 'shut your bone box'.
- Casket, coffin, wooden overcoat.

BARNACLE: (neo)

- Anything, or anyone bothersome, annoying.
- To be clingy: as a toddler wrapped about a parental thigh.

STEVE MORGAN

BUSTDOWN: (ODUE)

- (Colloquial) - Chicago gangster showdown.
- (Colloquial) - Promiscuous woman.
- (Vulg euphemism) - mammaplasty.

C:

C: (cee)

- Visually proficient.
- (Slang) $100.00 note.
- Grading: Second place to 'B'. Not much better than 'D'.

CABBAGE:

Taxi driver's unresolved issues.

CACTI:

- Gaudy neckwear.
- A <u>rope</u>.

CATCHFART:

A <u>bulldozer</u>'s sycophant, brown noser.

CATERPILLAR: (Auth orig neo)

Ancient version of a lazy-suzan. The rotating shelving of a colonnade placed at waist height of Temples (for votive offerings the deity could reach without having to step on, and be defiled by any earthen object), and/ or, any cafe/ bar outlet.

CALFSKIN:

Modesty suit for teenage bovine.

CANOODLE:

Smallest breed of toy poodle.

CAMPAIGN:

The irritation of outdoor activities.

CAMPERS/CAMPING: (OE)

(16c) team field sporting event. Believed to be enhancing of farmland.

CARRION:

Luggage.

CARRY-CASE:

Clothing. The fabrics that encase the flesh.

CONGRESS:

A <u>quorum</u> of politically aligned <u>elp</u> who meet to repeal legislation to ensure the continuance of their careers.

COKE-BOTTLE:

Thick-rimmed, thick-glass unattractive optic attachments. Esp., those that ensure the wearer is unattractive to the opposite gender.

CHINCHILLA:

Beardless.

COCKAMAMMY: (Auth orig neo)

Transgender chook. Is it now a hencock, or cockhen?

CATALYST:

- Moggy with a lisp.
- Feline aficionado of the musical talents of Franz Liszt.

CACKLING CHEAT:

chicken.

CONNOISEUR:

Narrow-minded specialist.

CADISH:

Little S.O.B.

CASHISH: (ODUE)

- Resembles legal tender.
- Loose change.

'CHAIRS':

Upperclass salutation.

CORONATION:

An art-form of pomp, and ceremony to affirm the personal belief of an elitist. Which confirms their believed divine right to be sovereign.

STEVE MORGAN

CRITICAL RACE THEORY: (neo)

A pseudo-theory, an illogical speculation, concept based upon supposition, and paralogism. Taught as 'fact' to the credulous gobbermouche without the offering of empirical evidences. Abbr. (CRT) is commonly believed by activist supporters as the ultimate inter-disciplinary 'examination' of how life, and groupings of persons have been adversely affected. Particularly, if that group is considered native to a region, and so is obviously marginalised by the majority who may, or not be of 'original' native genealogy. The native is uniquely disadvantaged by modern mechanisms of society. Supporters of CRT consider themselves 'enlightened' for the 'equity', and equality of all persons CRT espouses. The policies that are lauded as superior to any other. This theory has pervaded all aspects of society; from kindergarten, to the corporate boardroom. Politics, public service. CRT, essentially represents, and promotes a false 'victimhood'. The beginnings of CRT may have had noble reasoning. However, evidence is CRT has morphed into a refuge for activists, and supporters utilise to foster deep seeded race based <u>bigotry</u>. CRT hence, is a safe-haven for sectarian intolerance. It therefore should be treated with the same doubt as any other abstract idea that is devoid of much, if any empirical evidence.

COMMON:

- Not <u>unique</u>.
- Ordinary, predictable.
- Stigma of modernity.

COPYCAT:

- The startle a feline witnesses at a reflection in a mirror.

- A feline happy to hang out in a copy room making weird, obtuse duplications in compromising postures.

CLAQUE: (klak)

The soothing sound of one half of a railcar as it speeds along a rail-track.

CLICKERTY:

The other half of the soothing sound of a railcar as it speeds along a rail-track.

CATASTROPHE:

- Real bad lyrical poem.
- Wailing male feline attempting to court a mate.

CLAMMY:

Clam matriarch.

CHRISTIANITY:

See cult.

CLAMOROUS:

Impassioned, lustful mollusc.

CLIMATE CHANGE:

- Natural weather cycles, associated with nephology.

• Comprises one of the most illogical concepts, no doubt pilfered from the christian idea that to 'save' the planet, certain things must be sacrificed; I.e., it is proper to die that life is gained. According to 'climate' zealotry, it is more than ok that pristine ecology, and biodiversity is disrupted or destroyed 'for the greater good' of saving the planet by widespread use of 'green' sources of energy. Mass wind turbines, and farms of solar panelling that destroys productive land. Turning these areas into sterile patches. All are far from green. Having an approximated 10-15yr lifespan, are energy, and chemical intensive to produce, and are not biodegradable.

• (Modern alarmism) the grandest hoax of the twenty-first century. Fuelled by those claiming elite status who are heavily invested in the things touted as 'renewable' sources of energy. Holding goals and ambitions of population domination through high poverty, high costs, and subjugation of the masses. Consider: If the Earth were warming to unheard-of levels that are damaging to life, how the following is affected: (1) Incubation of animal life that begins with an egg. Are they incubated in polar regions, or, in warm waters, warm sands? (2) Why do plant, and animal life generally thrive in warmer/tropical regions (3) How many cities are built, and thriving in cold regions? (4) Why are politicians so thermophobic (afraid of heat), and determined to decarbonise, while installing energy intensive, inefficient sources of 'energy'. In denial of all forms of fossil fuels as an efficient source? (5) how have we allowed a tiny cabal of selfish, unqualified misfits to harangue and bully submission to their desires through fear, intimidation, propaganda, <u>misinformation</u>, <u>disinformation</u>, censorship?

• A climate answer: If she could speak she would say, all attempts to drive nature by way of force, I will rebuke you, I will rout all falsehoods, and refinements imposed that has kept me out.

CONDEMNATORY:

Living quarters of an <u>adversity</u> campus for students.

CONFESSIONAL:

• Seasoned scammer.
• An employed graduate of an <u>adversity</u> course.

CONTEXT:

Text messages informing a <u>confessional</u> of the next 'victim', client.

CAINITES:

• Those unfortunate lightless hours of high homicide rates.

• People group, ancestor of the Biblical Israelites. Often fought against, despised, and generally regarded as malcontented.

COWER:

Livestock breeder/ farmer.

CLIMATE VACCINATION: (Auth orig neo)

The attempt by governing officials, climate zealots, activists to reverse, or mitigate the mythically potential climate disaster - Global Warming.

By abolishing fossil fuels; coal, gas usage as a means of efficient, cost effective sources of energy. Those sources that have lifted millions from poverty.

CROCODILE:

- Crack phone call.
- Wrong number.

CROISSANT:

Furious insect.

CLINK:

- <u>Bootcamp</u>.
- Gullible German Commandant (Hogan's Hero's - American sitcom).
- Sharp ringing sound.

CANNER/CANER:

Willing participant.

COLANDER:

- Mutual land ownership.
- Housemate.

CATTLE:

Feline rattling play toy.

COOLTURE: (Auth orig neo)

The cultivating mood, and projection of those who believe themselves 'cooler than thou.'

COMMON GOOD:

- Once meant: For the benefit of the all. Serving the interests of all.

- (Modern definition) according to modern thought, including <u>political correctness</u>, <u>critical race theory</u>, freedom of speech, <u>truth</u>, Common Good must be reinvented to include, but not exclusively: curtailing, and making anything, and everything an offence. Making speeches, thoughts, writing, traditional beliefs, and empirical science knowledges; regardless if opinion, disagreement that is unspecified, abstract. Even ensuring the inanimate would likely offend or become offended, or abused for sensitivities were trampled. If the great Chinese military strategist, philosopher, Sun Tzu in his "Art of War" might have insisted on - "Common Good excellence consists of breaking all resistance to groupthink without aggression." ie., reforming laws, and statutes governing all aspects of life. Might this description therefore be outlawed as kind of hate speech? So, is not in standing with the groupthink of modern Common Good.

CANE:

Elder brother to Differently <u>able</u>. He one day decided, after becoming a mulligrub at his poor acting skills. during the disastrous rehearsals of a pantomime, to hand his brother 'the fuzzy end of a lolly-pop.'

Taking the lollypop Differently able soon fell with his 'face to the wall'. With great thought, and conviction about the proposals of better performances, Differently able soon joined the 'choir invisible', and was not heard of, or seen again. Presumed to be in heated skills training. Cane, afterward did suffer much 'Jobation'; punishment, and other debilitations at the wehrd of a deity. After, becoming banned completely from applying for any occupation as a 'walking companion', esp., for any Differently abled person. Including the infirm, elderly, and lonely. Soon, after sentencing Cane was forced to think with his legs, and absquatulated with his girlfriend. Reinventing himself as a knight. With his new knife, did settle in a distant land. Soon after becoming the owner of an Irish weirdo, - enoch. Inventor of all manners of knock knock joke silliness.

CHESTNUT:

(Vulgar) nipple.

COFFEE:

Cough tax.

CLUBBABLE:

- Formerly, bampuddler.
- Items easily belted for lack of resistance.
- The 'escapist' mood for want of entertainment.

CORN:

Real bad acted, produced pornography.

CONSPIRACY:

- Unauthorised persuasion of ideas.

- (Theories), <u>truths</u> yet exposed, confirmed.

- Labelled <u>disinformation</u>, and/ or <u>misinformation</u> before the recognition of being true. Often labelled as these by opponents who either know their own deceit, or are truely ignorant. Including <u>bulldozers</u>.

- A maladjusted art in deception.

CORNER:

- 'B' grade <u>corn</u> performer.
- Cereal crop producer.

CHURCH:

The asylum of the deluded, and/ or easily manipulated. Where a con-artist is employed to affirm all manners of misfortunes, either real but likely imitation, employing groundless rhetoric to rouse approval of idleness in mind, and an auto-votary. With weekly patronising spruiked, "Give me coin, and I will enjoy you."

CRYPTOZOOLOGICAL:

Academic <u>adversity</u> course that explores the viability of the 'cremation of mythical creatures, and phantasms.' Whether these actions are ethical, warranted, or possible.

CRYPTOGRAM:

Cremation ashes of a <u>cryptozoological</u> course are all weighed in cryptograms.

CHRIST:

The pseudo surname made famous by an ancient family of carpenters who organised a guild specific to that profession. The Christ in his spare time did on public holidays, festivals, weddings, bar/bat Mitzvah's, and several other religious festivals did entertain the ancient <u>Middle Eastern </u>regions. Showing off skills as a thaumaturge.

His prowess, and sense of fame, and importance soon overwhelmed all sensibilities. Becoming headstrong, his assumptions have rekindled a like desire among many celebrities, and peasants in equal measure. Leading them to all falling victim to a ruling class of authoritarians whom soon after-declared them cancelled. To this day, the Christ figure is revered as the exemplary of humankind. Despite near all being sick to <u>death</u> of his high-minded prattle. The Christ soon after being made a martyr for the cause of the guild. Being subjected to the pains of cancelling by <u>crucifixion</u>. He was then left alone for three days, but not forgotten about by friends. Suddenly, and unexpectantly he did make a celebrity appearance and beginning to encourage the dozen so illiterate Facebook followers to imitate his footsteps along the beaches; which unknown then had been washed away just three days prior, a cause that climate junkards claim as the result of rising seas.

The Christ did also make many promises while playing jump with his mates. When he had done suddenly jump so high, he did apparently disappear. Followers, and friend began earnest studying <u>nephology</u>; in a feeble attempt to locate their friend. Many autobiographies, and letters of pleading were penned in hopes to locate their friend. Many have survived to the present. The Christ has been lost now for over two thousand years. Yet, new followers, and search party's still study the autobiographies in their meeting places, called a <u>church</u>. Several, of the search party members prefer now the title <u>fishermen</u>. They hold a staunch faith that the Christ will eventually be found safe and well. Or, that he will reappear. When he does, the belief is his thaumaturge activities will resume. He will also graciously begin again his teachings. This time to the now millions of Facebook followers.

This 'Christ' offers the believer the illogical, and delusional view that in order to live, there must be <u>death</u>. Further, individual <u>life</u>, and death has been 'conquered' by a single 'mythical' entity. Yet, no man can die, or live for anyone else!

COLLAGEN:

Lineage of the Boarder Collie breed of canine.

CONSTERNATION:

Persistently over-bearing nation.

COURT:

You're nicked matey!

CONTEMPLATES:

Cheat cards, prompts used by amateur con-artists. Those in training.

CONTRABAND:

- Musical ensemble of bootleggers.
- Alternative musicianship.

CONTROVER:

Continental vagabond.

CORK:

Cockney accented stork.

COCCYX:

(<u>Bit</u> risqué) best not to proceed, as it may cause uneasiness with one's vestigial vertebrae.

CHASTITY BELT:

The oppression of sexuality committed against female slave-classes; halting experimentation, and copulation with a maid. Enforced by a male of the ruling class of yesteryear.

CRITICIZE:

The range of insect garment sizes.

CANDELMAS: (OE)

Religious service conducted by candle light, commemorating Earth day.

CONDOLE:

Double-dipping of social welfare benefits by deceit.

CRISIS: (Auth orig neo)

Health, food, energy, monetary, 'climate' crises; the mechanism employed by those who assume the right to control, manipulates, subjugate another. To weaken the world population for their own nefarious satisfactions, and ideologies.

CONDEMN:

Motto of a con-artist guild.

CUGGER MUGGER: (Irish)

Statement directed to the prized activities of those participants hanging about in bars, pubs, metabolic clinics, comfort stations, work places, religious institutes, parliament, or anywhere else that supports a congregation of individuals sprouting useless blabber.

CRONYISM:

Colloquial speeches of an olden bugger.

CHEVROSHANKS: (Auth orig neo)

Legs.

CONEHEAD:

• Martian race first introduced to the Earth in 1976 by Dan Aykroyd. They had elongated crania (cone-shaped), that housed a pea sized brain. Somewhat intelligent. Hyper-literal, and cousin race of another species - the 'Spock's'. Cone heads despite their oversized crania, are like their cousins mostly devoid of emotion.

- Dull, but intelligent human.

COUNTER-NOISE:

A device used to rouse the attention of a store clerk.

COUNTERPANE:

The irritating use of the counter-noise by customers.

COUNTERPOINT:

A whack in head, eye by a store clerk from frustration at the irritating counterpane. A direct result of the incessant use of a counter-noise by a customer.

CANCEL CULTURE:

- See, crucifix.
- No manifestation of human achievement.

CURSORY:

Creche where toddlers are schooled in the art of swearing.

CROSSCOUNTRY:

An angry sovereign State, providence.

CONSPECTUS:

A pamphlet detailing the means of scamming the next mark, victim.

CAPSIZE:

Pending the diameter of one's head.

CARPAL:

A forever grumbling sidekick always upset over inconsequential matters.

CARPET:

- Animal companion that persistently whines with anxiety when left alone.
- A pet most contented when snuggled on the parcel shelf of a vehicle.

CRACKERJACK:

Mechanical device to raise broken biscuits.

CATEGORY:

Bloodthirsty, violent feline.

CUBICLE:

Rough mode of early transport.

CRYSTALISE:

Twenty twenty vision.

CRUCIFIX:

- Non negotiable religious punishment.
- Primitive, crude serious, and debilitating form of persecution.
- Harshest form of cancel culture.

CANTALOUPE:

Opposite to <u>absquatulate</u>.

CARPENTARY:

- Incarceration of unruly, maladjusted fish.
- Impound lot for unruly vehicles.

CATSHID: (OE)

(Vulg) feline excreta, stool.

CATTLEGATE: (OE)

An investigation into the truth of squatting cattle on <u>geep</u> paddocks. A 16th century practice that was deemed unlawful.

CYNIC:

A realist valuing <u>truth</u> above fancy.

CYCLOPS/CYCLOPIAN/CYNOSURE:

- (Metaphysical) singleminded.
- Stubborn.
- Primitive understanding.

- An attention seeker.
- To concentrate, have a single focal point, or emphasis.

CHANGERWIFE: (OE)

- Female swindler.
- Feminine chameleon.
- Wandering wife, of a swinging <u>relationship</u>.

CHEESE, (Grene): (OE)

Immature dairy.

CHOPIN BLOCK: (OE)

The annoying mental block encountered by composers, and musicians.

COLLECTIONEER: (OE)

Relieved pauper. Having been 'purchased' and so saved from a life of destitution on the streets.

CHEESE PRESS:

- Exercise equipment for podgy dairy products.
- Dairy commentariat.

COLLECTOR OF THE POOR: (OE)

- Employee of a <u>collectioneer</u>.
- Professional hobbyist/ accumulator of the downtrodden, the exploited.

CREATION MYTHOLOGY:

An ideology still revered by god-mythologists. That a deity or other nondescript entity at sometime in a distant past burped, farted, spoke what was on the mind. Therefore, causing the immediate materialisation of physical objects from nullity.

CARFAX:

Portable fax machine.

CRI DE COEUR: (Fr.)

Crying, pleading heart.

CREATION SCIENCE:

Oxymoron.

CRACKCOWES: (OE)

Drugged livestock.

CREED:

Trumped up contradictory set of statements, values, and regulations organise by a cult hierarchy. Ensuring the forcing of compliance for maintaining a right standing within the cult society.

CULT:

An organised obsession, persuasion, movement, or guild, or community of likeminded persons. Holding to beliefs that are smaller than those held by the wider society.

CUFF N' STUFF:

Arrested.

CRIOSPHYNX:

Grecian imitation of the Egyptian sphynx. Sports a rams head.

CRYPTOGENUS/CRYPTOGENIC:

Unknown relations.

D:

D: (dee)

- Most certainly a grading of poor quality in comparison to 'A', 'B', and even 'C'.

- The saloon deck of the Titanic, (Lower deck).

- To mark a well-oiled, rat arsed, blotto fool.

DEAD WAGON:

Hearse.

DUFFER:

An idiot deserving to be stuffed into a gunny/ pouch.

DEINOSOPHIST:

Skilled, and conversational dining table.

DUMB:

The most intellectually challenging of all words. Immediately after beginning the pronouncing of this word, *um* causes the speaker to slightly pause. Leaving 'B' hanging and ultimately forgotten.

DOODLESACK:

- (Scot) Bagpipes.
- (Vulg. Auth orig neo) men specific britches.

DOOMSTER: (Auth orig neo)

• Where all failed predictions of gloom are sent after times for their occurrence passes.

• Old Testament, modern predictors of calamity.

• <u>Abnormis Sapiens</u>: just as Roman Lyricist Horace called those lacking wisdom, and knowledge aside own fears, and projections.

DOOMSURFER:

To imbibe obsessively upsetting, catastrophic news stories. Turning the reader into a full-fledged <u>doomster</u>.

DREAMFISH:

Psychedelic water creatures.

DANDIPRAT:

Juvenile dandelion.

DECIMATE:

One tenth of <u>mateship</u>.

DRAGGLE:

Flamboyant prattle of a parodic performer.

DAMNIFIED:

Not quite stupefied, just a little alarmed.

DEFETED: (Auth orig neo)

The dramatic result of the Third Law of Motion being forced upon your person by another prat. Where, static equilibrium is tested, by being whacked, shoved, or pushed to the point that stability is compromised, and undermined severely. To become so weakened that there is a bout of suffering of declension, causing <u>basiphobia</u>. The result of either <u>abigail</u>, or other knucklehead.

DOMINATRIX:

Dominating partner of fornicating friends.

DACTYOLOGY:

Sign language.

DEMORALISED:

Turning to <u>advice</u>.

DISINFORMATION: (Modern 21st century)

Factoids deemed as propaganda. Championed, and spread by government, and opponents. Often used out of context, and coupled with <u>misinformation</u>. Specifically, used to stifle, berate, disrupt debate.

DISCURSIVE:

Negating old fashioned cursive script style of writing in favour of PRINT.

DEFAME:

Truth to one. A dishonesty for another.

DEFENESTRATE:

- Defence magistrate.

- To bugger off out a window; either forced, or voluntarily.

- To discard a wrapper; musical, or confectionary, from an automobile aperture.

DICTIONARY:

- Elocution aid.

- <u>Abetter</u> way of learning the significance of <u>wehrds</u>, and their meaning. Teaching the reader the value, and usefulness of definitions.

- A canary trained to execute betterer elocution.

DISAPPOINTMENT:

Precedes <u>opportunity</u>.

DYING CHAMBER:

Hospice, nursing home.

DELUGE:

The rage of a deity after knocking over a pitcher of water. Causing widespread dismembering of the human population from existence because of the following maelstrom.

DELIGATE:

Big Cheese scandal - the blue vein files.

DOGMA:

A bitch.

DOGFISH:

Small carnivorous fish patrolling your swimming hole, pool to stop unauthorised entry.

DENOTE:

- To steal legal tender.
- To destroy minutes of a meeting.

DIGESTATE:

Carrying twin fetuses.

DISINFECTANT:

An insect cleared with a clean bill of health.

DISQUIET:

Raucous.

DISCOMBOBULATE:

Fun way to flummox, perplex, baffle, gravel, mystify, or simply confuse, and puzzle an audience.

DOGFISH

DEFLATION:

Flatter inflation.

DESIGNING:

Removal of advertising.

DELIGHT:

- To switch off artificial agents of illumination.
- The twelve hour period called night.

DENUDE:

To put your <u>carry-case </u>back on.

DEVILISH:

A little inappropriate.

DECEMBER:

Only thirty more disappointments remaining in a <u>year</u>.

DECEPTION:

Celebrating the final day of <u>December</u>.

DEATH:

- Interchangeable with the more pleasant term, sleep. The natural process of unconsciousness. Occurring during the lightless hours when the human body best repairs.

- The permanent catatonic state experienced by all life forms - the Big Sleep In.

DIFFICULT:

A faith community, movement of contrasting, contradictory, unrelated persuasions.

DISAFFECTED:

The <u>trifecta</u> is reversing in lethality.

DARK AGES:

The period following the fall of the Roman Empire to Christianity. A time little understood for most of world-knowledge, and practices of civilised societies till that point was either assimilated or destroyed or declared an abomination by the 'new' order. Modern twenty-first century society is emerging through another dark age. An age of political correctness acting in similar fashion to early Christianity. Instead of torturing through physical means as the Inquisition had done to opponents, the new religion of the politically correct woke, cancel through social media, banking, and other means to de-person their detractors. The religion of the woke does deny most standard knowledges; scientific truth, biology, and several vital atmospherical elements are declared harmful to life, so are consciously demonised to satiate a minority. Those who desire to control, manipulate, coerce, subjugate the majority. Leaving them in poverty, while the minority rule in opulence. Just as Papal edicts, and much of church doctrine thrusts upon believers.

DISSIPATE:

Opposite to anticipate.

DIET:

- Waist management through suppression.

- The obsession of a large portion of Western societies that enriches the opportunists who exploit the feebleminded, and human dustbin, gutbucket.

DECENTRALISED:

To blind a cyclops.

DREAMS:

Dreams lead to ambition. Nothing destroys dreams, the sense of purpose, destiny more than; physics, reality, gravity, your physical, and mental aptitude, self-delusion, <u>bureaucracy</u>, government autocracy, legislation, your opponent's and other like issues.

DELIBERATE:

To incarcerate.

DEMISTER:

A medical procedure, operation to make someone a eunuch.

DEMYSTIFYER:

The specialist who performs the medical procedure to transform those wishing to <u>demister</u>.

DAYBREAK:

- Daylight criminal behaviour.
- The breach, fissure, fracturing of dawn.

DIRTY WORDS:

- <u>Oxymoron</u>.

- Those expressions, writings, speeches, statements, remarks that are held unacceptable. Despite being formerly accepted.

- Any expression etc., deemed offensive, inappropriate to the <u>woke</u>, <u>puritan</u>.

• A soiled well-worn word-finder <u>dictionary</u>.

DREADNAUGHT:

No fear, or apprehension.

DOCTRINE:

A <u>creed</u>.

DUMBPHONE:

Not a 'smartphone'. A device that is used as an old-fashioned mobile telephone only. When the mobile telephone was first released, it was deemed a 'brick' for its cumbersomeness.

DOUBLETHINK:

The dysfunctional mental processes of an <u>elp</u>, or other likeminded person whom through their own justified reasoning accepts an injustice; exploitation, suppression, inequality, or platitude. While contributing to those very injustices.

DISTORIAN:

The manipulative <u>disinformation</u> of a history claimed as factual.

DROOLWORTHY:

The ogling of someone deemed extremely attractive. Often causing the infatuated to salivate like a <u>groaking</u> canine.

E:

E: (e)

The key to making sense of the following nons^n^cical int^llig^ntly r^adabl^.

- ^thi^rstill th^ ^xplanation for all ^arthlings could b^ ^th^r^al forms of ^nglish^s.

- A Frenchman wrote an entire book without using 'E'. Translated into English as 'The Void.'

- Second-rate merchant ship, designated by 'E'.

- 'E' - the earliest known designation for 'pi'.

- 'E' - the most used of letters of the alphabet.

ENGLISHES:

Lashings of common dialect.

EXECUTOR: (OE)

A will enforcer.

EARWORM:

The most annoying melody that suddenly appears. Reverberating through your head, and mind, vexing your thoughts. The melody is likely to be least likeable. Yet, for an unknown reason your mind has seen fit to inflict upon you its most narcissistic personality. The sole purpose is to drive you crazy.

EARTHLING:

A newly forming planetary body. Showing the characteristics for the potential to supporting life.

EAST:

- Not <u>north</u>, <u>south</u>, <u>west</u>.
- (Metaphysical) symbolises hope, and inspiration.

ENCYCLOPEDIA:

Disease of one eye.

ELEPHANT BIRD:

Avifauna with a prehensile appendage.

EXPERT:

Spirt under pressure.

EXCRUCIATORS:

- Tight, painful '<u>beetle crushers</u>'. Often high heeled, stiletto's worn by women and the <u>bag-drag.</u>

- Blister causing footwear.

END:

- Das Nichts. Nothingness, zip, zero, nuddah, demise, death.

• According to modern hysteria, mankind, the Earth is 'at boiling point'. People are dropping dead in the street (from extreme heat), and if not addressed immediately by the population, our own das nichts, extinction is imminent (according to the U.N.).

ENDING:

• Continued das nichts. Nothingness.

• Everything has an end. Regardless, how long, short, or indifferent a life. An ending is always unexpected. It is pointless; therefore, as the god-mythologists claim, to strive, believe, hope for a continuation of life in another realm. Mankind must then accept that no man can die for him; no man can live for him. Life, and death is the constant necessary for a continued balance equilibrium.

• Only sausages have two endings.

ENDLESS:

Infinity?

EIGHT:

When seven eight nine, ten was left hungry.

EMU:

See ostrich.

ENDLESS:

Extended continuation.

ELECRIVERSION: (Auth orig neo. Elek-tra-vurshun)

Showing, holding an aversion, hatred, mistrust, suspicion of electrical devices, such as the <u>dumbphone</u>.

ET CETERA:

The expression used by writers, speakers to fool their audience into believing there is more to the point being made.

EXHORTION:

To encourage a <u>corn</u> performer to depart the <u>corner</u> industry.

ENTOMIC:

Keyhole surgery of the intestines of a creepy-crawly.

EXPENSIVE:

Removal of a preoccupation.

ECLAIRCISE:

- Fitness regime for those podgy sweet treats.
- A religious purging ritual for dispelling a confectionary addiction.

ECLOSION:

"It's alive, It's alive." exclaimed Frankenstein at the reanimation of moth pupa.

ELP: (neo)

A trickster, evader of responsibility.

ECTYPE:

A genre of modern film:

- Duel.
- Terminator.
- Robocop.
- Bladerunner.
- Ex-Machina.
- Humans.

ELFIN:

- Boisterous.

- A dorsal fin of an elderly elf that makes them look hunchback out of water, and a shark while swimming.

EGO-RAMP:

Rostrum, Dias, platform from which to be long-winded, self-aggrandising, noisome for the purpose of aggravating another person with constant blabber.

EXHORBITANT:

A satellite, or insect astronaut in a descending orbit.

EYE-OPENER:

Mechanical device to gently pry open an encrusted eye after contracting an eye disease.

F:

F: (eff)

- The most feared, and well-known letter of the alphabet.

- An immediately understood vulgarity: "f... off", "f... you, you crazy..."

- Completely rejected, graded 'F' - FAIL, FAILURE.

- To cause, or participate in a rumble in a religious institute once caused you to be branded with an "F".

FAVICON: (Auth orig neo)

- A well executed, and lucrative scam that a con artist has perfected, and so is their favourite con. Melding of Favourite + con.

- (Modern) denotes favourite *icon*.

FARTOWN:

- West Yorkshire (U.K.).
- An odorous village.
- Very distant from here.

FORESEEABLE:

- The 'prophetic' gift of witnessing an event, or situation before it materialises.

- Intuition.

FORGIVEABLE:

- Premeditated emotional support.
- Intentional Sacrifice.

FOREVER:

The continued extension of existence before all this torture freezes over.

FART FILLERS: (neo)

Any <u>carry case</u> covering the lower portion of your body that bears the brunt of your backdraft.

FABULOSITY:

When a myth inadvertently strays from intrigue.

FISHERMEN:

- Mythological water deities.
- Assigned name of <u>church</u> membership.

FERRET:

Thief.

FREELANCER:

Promiscuous person.

FOLDEROL: (18c.)

A <u>wehrd</u> that is one of those olde worlde terms. A lively expression sure to <u>discombobulate</u> for it's showiness.

FUTURE:

- The future is the moment directly following the completion of this sentence.

- Is always beyond the immediate <u>now</u>.

FUNGONEGELICAL: (Auth orig neo - fun-gon-gelikal)

Those fundamental religious believers who show limited, or no sense of gaiety regards many circumstances of life. Those who persist in the pursuit of their ideological belief with a bordering hysterical fervency, while also continuing to proselytise the <u>puritan</u> ideology.

FACSIMILI:

Similar but not quite naked <u>truth</u>.

FORMALDEHYDE:

Quick! Hide all documentation. The Fuzz are here.

FORGETFULNESS:

A gift of a deity as compensation for insolvency of mind.

FRIENDSHIP:

Not a <u>warship</u>.

FIVE ESSENTIAL FOOD GROUP HIERARCHY:

According to modern 21st century groupthink/ politics, for a society to flourish the Five food group hierarchy must now represent as an inverted pyramid:

- Climate change.

- L.G.B.T.I.Q.A. + agenda.

- Gender reassignment/ acknowledgment.

- Woke adherence, (and the balancing point).

- Food, and other necessities, essentials, cost of living stability, and honest governance. Only, if these are least costly.

FREE:

No longer detained, or controlled by another. Like wealth, there is no cost to being free. Acknowledge, and live in it now, or strive for more but never quite reach the ideal. There is no cost to the freedoms already gained.

FOXTROT:

A piaffe competition for carnivores.

FEAR:

• Is foremost an illusion. Like a room of mirrors; which reflection is the real you?

• Is the inhibitor of innovation, intrigue, initiative.

• Is the least understood psychological condition of any citizen. Effectively used by those claiming elite status. Fear, is the weapon of choice for those in the field of mind control, manipulation, coercion, and mind propaganda. Fear is used to destabilise, disarm, manipulate populations. For instance, how easy was it for governments to control populations over the recent (2020-2022) Covid pandemic; through QR codes, movement monitoring, curfew, mandated medical intervention (vaccines), and various other suppression, and controlling tactics. All accomplished through fear.

FLIES:

• Where do they all come from?
• What is their purpose?

FAINTING:

Barely visible artwork.

FARCE:

Very quick.

FARTHER:

Distant patriarch.

FLATTER:

Much less buoyant, circular than previously.

FLESH-POT:

Zombie ceremonial cauldron.

FIRE:

After submitting to domestication duties, fire became the main source of curing ills caused by uncooked foodstuffs. Like jubjub, <u>jackaroo</u>, and other victuals that is best served hot. Fire, also served as underfloor heating, of water for bath tubs, and general cave flooring. Serving also as an illumination device, driving hide-n'-seek games to become a past-time, and cutting down the scare/surprise tactics of the homicidal. Fire, did become an effective tool for illuminating artistic impressionism. Particularly, for the talented who worked on the walls of caves, and other darkened areas for fear of punishment of fellow citizens. Because, their skills were not recognised as 'telling the whole story' properly. Over many years of neglect, many of these works of art, and murals have fled for exposing their own reflection. Those that chose to stay upon the cave walls are now recognised by modern peoples as great works, and wonderful <u>faintings</u>.

FLIRT:

Little fart.

FOUL-MOUTHED:

Resembling a bird that utters profanities.

FORTITUDE:

The reinforcement that was meant to safeguard workers on the Ancient Landmark, known to moderns as the Eiffel Tower of the Middle East; the Tower of Babel high-rise. The fortitude failed dramatically; however, causing much consternation, and swearing blather by the immigrants employed. Such blathering of many tongues caused great confusion with worksite Forman.

FRIDIGIOUS: (obs, 1630)

So cold, horripilation becomes extremely hostile.

FUMIGATE:

Extremely obnoxious barrier requiring sanitation.

FOOT FACELIFT:

A kick to the face.

FLESH TUB: (OE)

The human, animal body; the casing snugly holding the innards.

FOR FREE/ FREE GIFT:

Tautology.

FREEDOM OF RELIGION:

The contorted sense of right that permission is granted to one accepted god-mythologist's creed, allowing them to conduct, and infiltrate, and harass another in manners it deems to fit. Those over and above the feelings, beliefs, thoughts, lives of any other creed of world god-mythology. While a separate god-mythology is able to inflict grievous bodily harm upon an opponent for being opposite in thought, belief, conduct. Particularly, if sensibilities are determined to have been stomped. All in the safety of knowing there will be no coming consequence, or retribution.

FREEDOM OF SPEECH:

Just as <u>freedom of religion</u>. Freedom of speech is the freedom that bands of minority institutes, groups, <u>cults</u> possess. Allowing permission of those groups to conduct themselves in a manipulative manner using propaganda; through <u>political correctness</u>, harassment, bullying, slander, to accuse the historic past, a future point, or a present moment of being insensitive, thoughtless, hateful, inconsiderate of a 'sacred cow', a snowflake entity, an accepted minority ideology. Thus, they must be cancelled, torn down, rewritten, and <u>brainwashed</u> to believe the precepts of a minority. Including acceptance of their morals, and ethical standards as the fairest, most legitimate standard of practice. To dismiss these as legitimate requires retribution, treaty, and other grovelling. Despite the illogicality, and meaninglessness of any complaint and position held by the minority whiner.

G:

G: (gee)

- 'Naughty' — spot.
- 'G' string.
- Indicating gossip.

GRATITUDE:

- Highest altitude reached before bursting through and drifting off into space.

- Babel's fortitude.

- Most charitable.

GLISTEN:

Hearing with exuberant excitement.

GINGERBREAD:

Staple of red-heads.

GEEP:

A cross-bred sheep, and goat.

(The) GREAT reset:

A push by the faceless, unelected, unaccountable, bullies of world populations. Determined to control every aspect of the global population. A world-order concept for 'top-down' dismantling, restructuring, reassembling, redistributing, and re-imagining of world affairs; economic, personal, and other systems that currently operate on a global scale. These 'enlightened' one's, as they refer to themselves, wish to manipulate, coerce, control the deemed less equipped; mentally, financially, social classes of world populations. Their goal is to enact an 'enlightening' of the lower classes by essentially disempowering them of all wealth, personal control of their lives, livelihoods, education, foods, social acceptance mores by completely restructuring these to the benefit of the assumed 'elite' class. That the lesser classes, everyone else, are forced to become reliant on them for life, and purpose. Essentially, by forcing a transformation to subservience of the wealthy. Proposed by the socialist Klaus Shwab, of the WEF who meets yearly to discuss all manners of diabolic means to force compliance of world populations to their statutes. They desire to overhaul all world systems, replacing tralatitious principals with those the elite class deem worthy. Dictating the conditions, livelihoods, acceptabilities of the 99.99% of world populations. Their motto: "You will own nothing, and be happy."

Mao and other dictatorial personalities of world history have always attempted this scheming. It never fares well for the wider population. The world becomes economically, ethically, logically, morally bankrupt. Yet, modern populations and governments have been captured by such deceitful scheming and are heading full-steam ahead on their ludicrous mandates, either from ignorance, greed, or promise of greater personal wealth and power. There is among the elites a belief that they alone have a birthright, wealth-right, and the heritage of blood-right to dominate, subjugate, control we, the lesser class.

GALAGOG:

The state of being simultaneously awed, and unsettled by knowing the vastness of the universe.

GRANMARIAN:

Well-educated grandparent, adept in semantics.

GYROMANCER:

• The act of divination by rapidly revolving (as a spinning top) until falling unconscious. It is how the body remains contorted after becoming immobile after falling, determines the divine prospect.

• Often, a <u>University</u> student drinking game.

GAMBIT:

A little flutter on the gee, gee's.

GREATFUL:

See, <u>wasteful</u>.

GAY:

An eccentric, but jolly little word. It is a good thing to become foolishly gay every now and then.

GIANT:

• Imagined, mythical being of supernatural sizes, and physical attributes. A creature that embodies many religious, and folklore.

• Attributed sizes of several archaic, and modern plant, animal, and land and aquatic varieties.

- (Astronomy) much larger star system size and luminosity than our own.

- A great exertion of force.

- Anybody in bible times that was taller than the average height (5ft 10in). Esp., if they were differently Abel. Highly skilled. The most well-known 'Giant' in Western religion are the mysteriously named, <u>Nephilim</u> of Genesis 6:1-4.

- Persons with big personalities.

GUILT:

- Teenage feminine swine.

- (Modern) the inception of a previously unknown <u>syn</u> placed upon a person of a <u>cult</u>, called a <u>church</u>.

- The delusional state causing self-flagellation.

GENDER NEUTRALITY:

Either/or.

GRAVEN IMAGE:

A solemn, indelible representation.

GREEN ENERGY:

- Hoax.

- The failed granddaddy savior of climate zealotry.

- The swindle elites, and zealots utilise with the device of propaganda, manipulation, coercion to ensure a steady growth in their personal wealth creation while not lifting a finger to mitigate the crisis proposed.

GUBBLE:

Exploitable prattle.

GNAW:

Scottish - 'NO'.

GHOSTS:

The manifestations of inner dreads.

GODLING:

Inexperienced deity.

GROSER:

More disgusting than awful, bad, nasty.

GROWL:

Pissed-off owl.

GRAVE:

The funniest finale of the rich, famous, elite, and the hoi polloi for the grave yawns for all alike.

GOD PARTICLE:

(In physics) a god-particle is the elusive, and mysterious <u>bit</u>, subatomic element believed by scientists to represent the dandruff of a deity.

GROAK:

• Not related to amphibians. Cats, and dogs groak. Children groak, you groak, we all groak. Have you ever caught yourself groaking, but had little idea that this was what you were doing? Surely, at one point you found yourself staring into the oven salivating with the smell of roasting meat? Or, with desirous eyes impatiently awaiting the cake on the cooling tray? Maybe, you have noticed that every time you eat a snack outside, or the park your pet dog, or a flock of seagulls seems to harass you with their eyes. Hoping to gorge what you have? This is groaking. Groaking is an act of the eye.

• Groaking is essentially the featured pop song of the (1987) movie 'Dirty Dancing.' Performed by Eric Carmen, "Hungry Eyes."

• In modern parlance, 'groaking' has taken on a stigmatised persona; when a natural bodily function, such as sneezing, coughing without empirical evidence is vilified, and questioned, frowned upon regardless how harmless a cause.

GEHENNA:

Originally, this was a fire-pit where unwanted newborns, and other sacrifice's were made at an altar. Long before those practices were outlawed, and considered barbaric. Also, the place where the trashy, and garbage was incinerated, such as criminal bodies, as a means of 'space-saving' environmentalism. Ash taking less space than any burial. The fires of gehenna were unceasing, and so witnessed as the place of eternal torture. Which eventually, morphed into the abode of eternal fire, brimstone of the Christian concept of <u>hell</u>.

GNU: (gah'noo)

The subject of an hilarious tune created by Flanders and Swan: "I'm a GNU".

GOD'S MERCY;

Beloved greasy hangover breakfast of bacon, egg on toast.

GOD:

- Mythological life-force, sprite, id, spectre, ego, animating principal. Whether good, or spiteful, or indifferent. Believed by all religious mythologists to possess abilities of immortality, and other thaumaturgic practices. Is always an entity representative of the believer. A man, woman, plant, animal, or a hybrid of it. The celebration of this entity as a human being only eventuated in the last 2500years as also omniscient, omnipresent, omnipotent. Which are all mutually exclusive. To a modern mythologist believer this entity titled god, is the ultimate guiltwright. The one entity who has written a ledger of all deeds, good and bad of every human. The one who will use this ledger to determine through judgment, a person's worth sometime after their deaths.

- GOD - represents one of the most pervasive, secretive, and toxic elitist syndicates ever devised on planet Earth: the organisation of Guns, Oil, Drugs. An extremely powerful control mechanism of world affairs, and populations.

H:

H: (aich)

HABIT:

<u>Bit</u> of laughter. The short expelling of air at the very beginning of a spontaneous expression of amusement.

HUMBLEBRAG:

The self-deprecating boaster.

HOT-BLOODED:

Mammal.

HUSBANDMAN:

(21st. c) an acclimatised male partner of the household. Comfortable with domestic tasks. Mostly, without seeking how, or what utensil, and tool best used for a kitchen task.

HYPHONATION: (Auth orig neo)

A high-pitched production, utterance, speech, or other sound.

HALITOSIS:

A disease of the mouth, foot breath. Occurring after putting your foot in the mouth during a conversation.

HATCHERY:

Incubation chamber.

HORTICULTURE:

Customs, traditions, lifestyle praised by the promiscuous.

HORTATORY:

- Alternative club of the promiscuous.

- School for the interested in learning melodramatic's, and like professions.

- Living quarters for the practical placements of houghmagnandy students; those practical studies of adulterous activities.

HORSPITAL:

Equine spittle.

HOSIERY:

- Firefighting equipment storage unit.
- Hospice of the foolish, uncultivated mind (a hoser).

HERMAPHRODITE:

- (Olde worlde) a six-wheeled cart.

- (Modern) the evolution of the cart into ute, small-medium, heavy haulage vehicle.

- (21st c.) "Boys will be girls, girls will be boys. It's a mixed up, muddled up world..." by pop group, The Kinks. Lyrics to - 'Lola.' Is this life imitating art, or, art imitating life?

HAIRBALL:

Feline equivalent to the human ball game, poison ball. Played with a ball of wool.

HEKISTOTHERM: (heh-kis-toe-therm)

Extreme frigid temperatures at mountain peaks cause all hikers to canoodle each other's feet to save from severe frostbite.

HELLACIOUS:

The attitude adopted by residents, and staff of the underworld. Instead of care, staff and residents carry out their time with ferocious malice, and animosity.

HOPLITE:

- Low alcohol beverage.

- Light-weight Ancient Greek warrior.

- The calcified remains of a prehistoric marsupial with weakened development of hind-limbs.

HERETIC:

A cynic, or other holding to olde worlde beliefs, practices in preference to those held by a church.

HERPETOLOGIST:

A reptile, or amphibian with a Ph.D., in the Humanities. Majoring in studies of the human species; including classical arts, classical literature.

HELMET:

Meeting the devil after death.

HAMLET:

- Piglet.

- Stage production of the famed Shakespeare; a tragedy of a small goods producers of the sixteenth century.

- Village, birthplace of small goods producer 'Don'. Oh, 'don' is good.

HANKER-CHIEF: (Auth orig neo)

Leader of desires.

HOLY WATER:

- An impossibility. Attempting to bore, or cause an aperture by burrowing through a body of liquids is futile.

- Oxymoron.

HATRED:

An aversion to anything scarlet, claret coloured.

HATE SPEECH:

Any opinion, act, thought, belief that is not supported by mainstream groupthink. Particularly, any of these that are deemed by 'the group' to contain <u>disinformation</u>, <u>misinformation</u>, or any rhetoric that could inadvertently offend the sensibilities, thought, belief of those enamoured with groupthink.

HOMELETICS:

Backyard olympics.

HISTORIAN:

- An accounting of gossip. Particularly, of those who claim significance.
- He who is great at telling stories for why he is home late, again!

HUMBLE:

Low-frequency expressions, articulations or sound.

HYPOCRICIDE: (Auth orig neo - hi-pok-riside)

- The hypocrisy of those who advocate for diversity, and other <u>politically correct</u> outcomes of all life, while announcing in those statements their own political incorrectness.

- A disease of the Socialist/ Communist, Globalist, Left-wing politician, activist. Gloating about an assumed 'lack' witnessed in the acts, words of an opponent, while being utterly blinded by their own <u>bothsideness</u> being simultaneously exposed.

HELLO:

• Traditionally, the underworld. Place of the damned. Place of infernal torture with hot-pokers, and other religious dismembering methods, and apparatus' delightfully dreamt by sadistic god-mythologists. A place inaccurately believed to be somewhere below our feet. But, should be realised to be 'the here, and now', for humankind tends to inflict upon any opponent to a cherished cause, the most hellish forms of existence devised.

• The apprehensive exclamation blurted at being able to comprehend with clarity <u>telephone</u> ventriloquism.

HYPER:

A religious performer (priest, worship leader) who uses sermons, or emotional manipulation, and stimuli to heighten enthusiasm, and response of chanting praise.

HAGGLE:

Cackling old hag.

HALF-PENNY:

One sided coin.

HAMPER:

The gentle swooning sound a satisfied, contented swine makes lazing about the window sill, or near a fireplace.

HANAPPER:

Chuckling while still asleep.

HASSOCK:

Novelty, jovial foot garments.

HICCUS DICCUS:

The full Roman Centurion name of the father of Brian - (movie) Life of Brian.

HOGWASH:

Walk through bathroom facility for swine.

HOMER:

The Simpson's favourite character, and beverage.

HOMOMYNOUS:

Self-conscious about coming out.

HORRID:

Street-worker homicide.

HORSELITTER:

Equestrian apples (waste).

HEATHENISH:

Somewhat antagonistic.

HEIROPHANT:

An enormous plant eating mammal with a prehensile appendage possessing extraordinary knowledge of mysteries, and the wisdom required to offer explanations.

HAIRSUTE:

Cousin 'iT' - Adam's Family.

HOARY HISTORONICS:

Ancient form of entertainment performed at a Colosseum.

HUMECTANT:

Sponge.

HELOTAGE:

Serf's up in ancient Sparta.

HADES:

Gehenna.

HYPOCRITE:

Those who despise all virtues while securing praise, and respect for what is execrated.

HANDGUN:

A mechanical device invented for the sole purpose of inflicting grievous bodily harm, and damage. Or, causing others to remain in a permanent catatonic <u>breathless</u> state.

HELL:

- The wonder if delight of the religionist that enemies, and other disliked persons are housed there for a very long duration. No parole, no appeal, no rehabilitation ever being granted, <u>forever</u>.

- The mythological folkloric accommodation block used to frighten, manipulate <u>cult</u>, or <u>church</u> members to stay the religious obedience.

- The <u>hello</u> world.

- <u>Gehenna</u>.

I:

I: (eye)

• Using both I's = twenty twenty vision.

• The most selfish of pronouns. 'I' is the subject, and object of brashness, self consciousness, and esp., the ego.

• Lowercase 'i' would look odd, naked without the tittle bouncing upon its <u>north</u> most point.

• Lowercase 'i' received the tittle, bouncing, balancing point in compensation of its size.

• The less the pronoun 'I' is used, the less likely a user is to suffer angina.

• The very first word learnt, used, spoken, and thought by a mind.

• The first thought expression of affection.

INFANS:

• A little infantile latin is child's play.
• Ingrown dorsal fin.

INKLING:

The tiny dot, full-stop mark made on paper.

IMMIGRANT:

Deluded <u>controver</u> believing any <u>alienation</u> must offer better, superior solutions to life than their own native patch of gravel.

INFINITY:

- (Philosophy) has no desire to fit in.

- Infinity, or 'endlessness' how long, short, large, or small is it? Is infinity truely endless, and how would we know? The concept of infinity is boundless as a theorem. Does infinity witness everything; the past, present, and future simultaneously? Is it always directed to all points. Can it be directionless? Is it never, but always? Infinity - the theorem that is all, but none. Converging at all points, and in all directions. Yet, who is to say infinity exists, while not existing?

ICHTHYOID:

- <u>Fishermen</u>.
- Having the look, and mannerisms of fish.

IDEOGENY:

A study of the family tree of ideas.

INFLATION:

- The cause, money.
- Opposes flatter.
- A cause of reckless governance.

INCOME:

Confused!

INCLUSIVITY:

An act of <u>political correctness</u> that is claimed as the exclusive right to vilify at will, with a <u>barrage</u> of nonsensical edicts, and corrections to long-held, verified truths of <u>reality</u>, science, and biology, or any other long-standing premise of life. Such inclusivity excludes all known logical premises to not offend the sensibilities of someone, or inanimate, or mythological thing, or entity. Those held by a select minority group. It is now discouraged to hold, or dare voice an objection to a 'progressive' viewpoint, regardless how illogical, insensitive, unreasoned, mythological. Long standing terms, phrases, beliefs are dismissed as not inclusive 'enough'. The reality of the modern conception of 'inclusivity' = a total exclusivity of anything humanity has enjoyed past, present, future. Unless, these are completely remoulded, restructured, and re-characterised. To disappear.

IMAGE:

The current obsession of the progressive generation. Those persons declaring themselves advanced in morals, and ethical standards. The 'I' personality loves blowing their own trumpet, insisting they be referred to by the first person singular. Surprisingly, even when their lives are entwined with another's.

IMPARTIAL:

Disobedient security, law enforcement officer.

IMAGINARY:

An aviary of stored inventory of favoured fanciful, phantasmal, hypothetical <u>real</u>.

IMPUNITY:

Unionised collective of troublemakers.

INDULGENCE:

An unenthusiastic flutter with narcosis.

INEPTOCRACY: (neo - in-ep-tokh-racy)

The system of governance where the least capable to lead is elected by the least capable of producing. Where members of a society least likely to sustain itself, or succeed are rewarded with goods, and services paid for by the confiscated wealth of a diminishing minority of producers.

INTERRELATED:

bloodline relations.

INDUSTRY:

A vacuum cleaner.

INFORMER:

They were something once, but are now something else.

INHERITRIX:

An heiress to the family brothel.

INQUISITION:

The 600year long ecclesiastical tribunal, <u>court</u> of those accused of heresy by the showy <u>puritan</u>. Beginning in the thirteenth century, by issue of an official castrating edict, <u>bull</u> of nonsense by Pope Alexander. The inquisition was never really formerly abolished, rather abandoned as a disciplinary device to grow congregations of the faithful with increasing crowds of the ignorant. The inquisition was however declared defunct in 1834, by Pope Paul VI. He recognised that this system of religious education would never succeed, for too many of its students soon after enrolling was found to have expired, or been excommunicated, or become inflicted with severe disadvantages.

Victims/students of this religious education order were initially charged with worshipping the wrong subjects, icons. Or, were studying the right topics in the wrong manner; I.e., inappropriately. It was deemed; therefore, nobody could save these wretched souls from the disciplinary actions metered. Many were sent to faggots piles, drowning, hot-poker games, yoga stretching, and body contortion exercises. Resulting in many lives being given up as these and the various other torturous exercises recommended was too extraneous to endure long-term. Unfortunately, no publicly appointed professional masseuse was in employment at the time. Only a well-paid amateur using the <u>heretic</u> as a spit-roast. They broke many Jewish laws of Passover, by intentionally breaking bones, ligaments. They caused widespread disemboweling, and other heinous punishments the religious order's own health ministers recommended, or when scrutinised, denied any knowledge regarding. Nobody fitted to disagree with the Pope, and the righteousness he declared as valid, and truthful to the wider populace. Half of these victims were declared, and labelled witches. A term Pope Innocent invented 200years after this religious schooling effort was established, and forced on an unsuspecting, uneducated society. It is recorded that upwards of 15million students of this system had their certificates of achievement terminated at the instruction of principal inquisitor's. An appalling indictment of homicide committed by god-mythologists who were under the assumed instruction of their Arch-deity.

IMBIBE:

Distillery of wisdom.

IMMACULATE:

The science of Parthenogenesis.

INK:

Substance used making writing on paper, and other surfaces legible. Rebellious Swine ingeniously use oink! To graffiti their stalls.

INLAWS:

Your unsuspected rebellious relative.

J:

J:

JACKAROO:

- Australian male marsupial who gatecrashes tents, and other human family gatherings; like, camping grounds. Either desiring an audience to satiate their own relevance deprivation syndrome, or purely by accident during a rumble with another outside clan member considered a total bastard by the mob.

- A Pom (Englishman) newly arrived to Australian shores.

- An occupant of the remote outback surveying Australia for no other purpose than employment, and experience during a 'gap' year, in readiness of completing studies of marsupial behaviour.

JILLAROO:

A lady Jackaroo.

JACKALOUPE: (1955)

- American mystical mammal suited to the lands of cryptozoology. Must be considered the perfect cryptogram candidate.

- Female accomplice absquatulating with her historian as his tenure of his former residence is cancelled.

JACKASSIFICATION: (1822)

A disease of the modern idiot.

JOLLYBOAT:

- Party vessel.
- Watercraft of most buoyant temperament.

JOURNALIST: (Auth orig neo)

Skilled in the artful use, and dissemination of gossip that serves public interests.

JE NE SAIS QUOI:

- What?

- (Literally) - "I do not know what."

- Whatever expression that is indescribable. Such as, "why are we here, and why are you reading this punishment."

K:

K:

- Symbol of the uneatable carat.

- Symbol of the chalk age. The age before blackboards were invented, - The Crustaceous Period.

- When in ancient Rome, never accuse falsely anyone. It will result in a a contribution of the 'K' brand clothing company.

- A distinctive cereal brand.

KIND:

A meaningless gesture claimed by sentient beings.

KNEE JERK:

The expressive explosive movement after becoming startled by a handgun while competing at a homeletics balderdash carnival.

KNIFE:

Better half of a knight.

KANGAROO WORDS:

That indecipherable language, lingo of the iconic Australian marsupial.

KANGAROO COURT:

Inconsequential hearings of the utterances of kangaroo words.

KNAPPING HAMMER:

- Rock crusher.

- A device for causing an instantaneous comatose state, potentially in readiness of surgery.

KNOWLEDGE BOX:

The casing of the seven pound grey matter between your jug handles.

KETTLE OF FISH:

Preferring mine fried, or baked. Boiling fish just renders a kettle unsuitable for the making of beverages <u>afterward</u>. Confused? You should be.

KNOWLEDGE:

Only worth a penny when able to be questioned, debated.

KALOLOGY: (khal-oh-loh-jee)

The first vocational beauty therapy course. Invented by Egyptian queen Cleopatra.

KAKIDROSIS: (kah-kid-ro-sis)

The cause, and desire to invent no-pong!

KEEP:

The inner stronghold where things you would rather hide away. These are safely stored, unexposed until unceremoniously exposed through violation, or invasion.

KISS-ASS:

Sycophant, groveller, willing door-mat.

KIDNAP:

Infant sleepy-time. Likely longer in duration than a nanna nap.

KNOCKER UP: (OE)

Slightly risqué. Sounding naughty, yet is quite tame. Was the occupation of someone in the 18th-19th century who was employed as a peeping-Tom. They went about tapping on windows of the unsuspecting in the early morning to wake the residence. In steady hope of frightening them from slumber; that they ready themselves for another gruelling day at the office. An occupation that preceded the invention of an expergefactor (alarm clock). Devices that no doubt was invented to drive homicide rates of these employees downward.

KNIGHT:

- Designated restful time.
- The burly partner of a <u>knife</u>.

KINGFISHER:

Supreme monarch of <u>fishermen</u>.

KOW-TOW:

Epitome of a <u>kiss-ass</u>.

KANTIKOY:

Practices of the pentecostal,and other god-mythologists as an expression of devotion, and adoration of their favoured entity.

L:

L: (ell)

LANGUAGE:

- The luggage of expression, and communication.
- Provincial idiolect.

LAPIDATE:

- To date a lap-dancer.
- A date under the influence of mind-altering substances.

LONGING:

Not a <u>briefing</u>.

LAMELESS:

Not infirm, deformed, incapacitated but healthy.

LIFESAVIOUR: (Auth orig neo)

Opposite to <u>unsavoury</u>.

LONGEVITY:

The unusual ideology allowing for a belief in an extension of the fear of death.

LOGOLEPSY:

Seize the word! From Gk., logos - word, + lepsy -to seize.

LONGNAMITY:

The supernatural ability to endure a injury while hatching revenge.

LABIOMANCY:

The skill of the deaf.

LOQUACITY:

• Verbose metropolis.

• Shortened medical designation of the disease Cacoethes Loquendi: verbal diarrhoea, gift of the gab. Often results in a diagnose of <u>halitosis</u>.

LIFE:

• The hustle and bustle before a visit from the realtor: Mr Grim, and his minion auctioneers.

• Happening while waiting to return to our own capuan comforts.

• The time spent inbetwixt expectation, and <u>disappointment</u>.

• The realisation that even the dopey are correct some of the time.

LORE:

Legalities of occulted, orc-ish knowledge.

LUNARIAN:

Labelling the residents of amun.

LOCUSTS:

All-expenses paid touring insect groups.

LYREBIRD:

Mischievous avifauna.

LUNATIC:

A manic disorder caused by too much luna observation. Ready attribute of werewolves, and other species who stare, and howl at amun.

LAMBASTE:

An irate geep.

LAMBENT:

Crooked geep.

LAMIA:

Lady mosquito with pointed canine teeth.

STEVE MORGAN

LAPPET:

Small canine companion happy to laze about your lap.

M:

M: (em)

- Movie: dial 'M' for murder - an Alfred Hitchcock production.
- Hindu: the dreamless state.

MACROCEPHALIC:

A <u>giant</u> with an immensely supernaturalist imagination.

MAGNETISM:

Describes those attracted to some iron-maidens. While being equally repulsive to others.

MARRIAGE:

Ecclesiastically sanctioned, <u>puritan</u> endorsed procreation. Enforced on the unsuspecting engaged in <u>horticulture</u>.

MATE:

Studies in practical <u>horticulture</u>.

MEA CULPA:

My 'Bad'!

MIDDLE AGES:

Waisted time spent in gastric studies.

MIDDLE EAST:

- To the Right of your breadbasket.

- Neither toward the <u>south</u>, <u>north</u>, <u>east</u>, or <u>west</u> of your position. But, smack in the centre.

MONOLOGUE:

An argument with yourself.

MIND:

Question: when you lose your mind, where does it go? Can it be retrieved, and restored to its former place?

MACHINATION:

Superpower of Terminators.

MYTHOLOGY:

The personal study conclusion to a religious premise, entity, conception. Compound: 'MY' + 'Theology'. Every Christian, or other religionist believer must conclude that their stated 'holy' texts, and folklore are mere 'mythology'. The written conclusion to a personal belief, understanding regards a religious premise.

MENDACITY:

A dishonest urban sprawl.

MAIL:

- Olde worlde communication services.
- A gender-neutral dude.

MAD:

The feeling that ensures the exasperated cry - damn!

MATTEROCRACIST: (auth orig neo)

New power structure where meritocracy is replaced by what is deemed to 'matter' more in importance; like, the ideology of the eco-warrior trumps the merit of scientific fact-based evidence.

MISINFORMATION:

Factoids that one side of an argument does not agree is valid. Often, labelled as <u>conspiracy</u> before evidenced as <u>truth</u>.

MAGIC:

An enterprise of fleecing coins from superstition.

MOURN:

That feeling a gloomy daybreak has at having to come into being.

MUSHROOM:

Sardine dilemma.

MAMMON:

World's longest serving trinity of earthen deities; the Great daddy, a Reserve Bank; the spiritual Temple, the Stock exchange; and the 'son' of these, local banking facilities. These three are more powerful, and desirous than any other religious <u>mythology</u>.

MASCULARA:

• Make-up, eye liner for males. Fashionable esp., in Egyptian provinces during the Pharaonic epoch.

• A popular fixture of Goths.

MONKEY:

• Shaped metal to fit the ward of a lock. Used on the days concluding sporting fixtures played during the weekend.

• Iron tool to wedge, and pry nails left in chalkboards after running fingers down them as an irritation to the ears.

MERCY:

Exclamation! Esp., upon being detected engaging in illegal, undesirable activity.

MESMERISM:

Trancelike posture after lapidation. Before the more popular, and respectably clothed designation, hypnosis.

MINE:

Only yours if you pry it from my person.

MERCHANT:

A Siren's call.

MEEKNESS:

Uncommon restraint to extract vengeance immediately.

MISTFORTUNE:

Lost,   excluded,   overlooked   wealth.

MESSIANIC

MULTITUDE:

Diagnosis D.I.D., (dissociative identity disorder).

MENOLOGY:

Studies on the impact of paternity.

MOUNTAINEER:

Quiet, the hills are listening.

MINION:

Small yellow tic-tac all male entity. Character of Despicable Me fame. Either cyclopian, or has two eyes. Wears a goggle/ goggles, black gloves, black boots, and blue cover-alls. Are mostly unintelligible, being childlike in behaviour. Are noseless, yet suffer effects of a fart gun. Have no discernible ears, but discern sounds. Are mostly bald, except a few strands of wispy hairlike strands. They are exceptional engineers. Minions are supposed to have been immigrants from Sweden. They are all biologically wired to serve the vilest villain, and become bipolar, and depressed if unable to serve in this fashion. They serve GRU- the terrible.

MATESHIP:

- Not a warship.
- Somewhere between friendship, and relationship.

MONONYMOUS:

Batchelor, spinster rodent.

MENDACIOUS:

Given to punishment, and other forms of <u>wehrd</u> play.

METALLURGY:

Allergic to all metallic minerals, and things.

MAMAMOUCHI:

- Groucho Marx's mother.
- The psychological, or physical pain inflicted by a parent when scolded.

MESSIANIC:

A manically messy teen.

METABOLIC CLINIC:

Cafe.

MASH POTATO:

Excreta deposited by a frightened ghost.

MOMENT:

A consequence of <u>infinity</u> that the human mind has conceptualised to <u>keep</u> madness in check.

N:

N:

NEBBISH:

- Somewhat timid. Easily frightened.
- Kind of nasal aperture presenting as a snout, or (neb) beak of a bird.

NEPHOLOGY:

- The trend of the environmentalist, global warming movement should be rebadged as a belief in building castles in the clouds. Many of their persistent predictions is the cloud-based religion of nephology.

- The back-up system of computer data.

NEPHILIM: (nefilim)

A word from the Old Testament, Genesis 6:1-4. The enigmatic chapter of Bible lore that has been butchered by Christian, and other religious scholars, authors in a feeble attempt to extract a meaning acceptable to a predisposed hypothetical mythology. Specifically, to the concept of a 'fallen mankind.' Tied closely to Genesis 3. Nephilim are supposedly a race of humanoid/hybrid angelic being. Savage, and possessing great strength, and other powers above humankind. According to the mythology of Genesis 6:1-4, a group of angel type entities disobeyed the deity and chose to mate with human women, producing the progeny, Nephilim. Current world-wide interest in U.F.O.'s and other mysteries, such as elongated skulls, huge skeletal remains have been used by Christian authors as props to their mythology of an angelic/ human hybrid. Bible lore is these creatures disobeyed a deity, were savage, and were responsible for pillaging, rape, and the ravaging of the earth in times past. The deity therefore had little choice than to cause a wide reaching flood (Noah, Epic of Gilgamesh) highlighting the devastation. Many issues and theories abound regards these entities:

Nephilim - is a transliteration, not translation of an ancient word to many means 'to fall'. Yet, is best translated to mean "mighty men/ warriors." The concept and emergence of these entities being related to the sinfulness of humankind comes from a misunderstood meaning of falling. The etymology of the word however is lost to time. Later Greek interpreters of the Jewish texts translated the strange word to mean 'giant'. Which, has morphed to only mean in modern times, large, huge, high.

Personal studies of these concepts over five years have concluded standard religious beliefs about Nephilim are flawed. If anthropological, scientific, religious, mythological, archaeological, and mystic beliefs, and interpretations are accounted for. Likely, Nephilim resembled the Neanderthal who interacted with the populations of the regions of the Levant. Genesis 6:1-4 is likely a condensed tale of interactions between these two people groups. The folklore that was eventually recorded when writing was invented. Modern religionists continue to manipulate, and doctor such tales for their own purposes.

NOW:

When is now? Why does now evade capture and detection when searched? Now is simply the most evasive time, for just when it is believed now is, suddenly now is removed and is no longer valid. So, what purpose could now serve? Now, is used often in phrase form; now, and then, only now, what now, and now for... yet, now certainly remains elusive aside our own belief as an adverb that announces a present moment, or a moment immediately following. Therefore, NOW must well, be now! Not then, or before then, or even after then. For, as soon as now is announced it vanishes. Anything prior, or after is too late, and too early for now.

NEIGHBOUR:

The one who persists encouraging disobedience to likability.

NAIL:

A neutered mail.

NEW TESTAMENT:

Old myths retold to suit abetter era.

NICOTINE:

To forcefully arrest a teen.

NEPOTISM:

To appoint or employ a favoured relative to undertake tasks you cannot be bothered completing yourself.

NORTH:

- Not west, or east.
- Above the summit of anything south.
- (Metaphysical) representing the intellect.

NARCISSUS:

The twitter chamber.

NOCENSE:

Poor.

NOISE:

- A fart that reaches the ear canal.
- The clamour of civilisation.
- Undomesticated music.

NIMBUS:

Agile transport.

NUDNICK:

Arrest a nudist.

NOOSPHERE:

The state of wisdom attained through consciousness, mind, and interpersonal relationships.

NECESSITARIAN:

- Grocery outlet.
- Earth closet, thunder-box, comfort station.
- Modern amenities.

NOMINEE:

Favoured lower-limb joint.

NONSENSE:

Objections, and complaints about the misuse, or abuse of <u>wehrds</u> in this <u>dictionary</u>.

NOSE:

• Sundial of the face.

• Verandah of the mouth.

• Agent of the body voted least likely to gain <u>asent</u> for persistent intrusion of another's affairs by psychologists.

NOVEMBER:

The penultimate weariness of a <u>year</u>.

NUCLEAPHOBIA (BIC): (Auth orig neo.)

A malignant disease infesting the mind, and will of many <u>bulldozer's</u>, and environmentalist activists/ terrorists. Stating that nuclear forms of energy production are unsafe, expensive. Because the <u>earworm merchant</u> of renewable sources; I.e., wind, and solar, is more efficient to build their wealth, and power over the plebs of a society. Such reasoning has become a <u>parasite</u> imbedded into the emotional faculty of the brain.

NITRATE:

Time, and a half pay rate paid for services of the <u>horticulturalist</u> promiscuous faculty.

O:

O: (oh)

OOFTISH: (oof-tish)

Tune by ABBA - 'Money, money, money.'

OPEC:

A band of countries with a <u>god</u> complex, displaying a lust for all things crude.

OPEROSE:

Oh, the effort, the effort.

OLDISH:

Neither young, nor old. Rather, as goldilocks, and porridge, might be just right.

OVERPOPULATION:

A myth concocted, and disseminated by the wealthiest 0.01% of world populations who desire that a reduction, and maintenance of the entire world population is curtailed to 500million. The notion of, and proposals to depopulate the world is the encouraging of <u>wars</u>, <u>God</u> strategies, many environmental laws to curtail agriculture, food production, 'new' food sources, and many medical practices.

OTHERWISE:

That's them over there.

OUTCOME:

Confused?

OUTDO:

- To ignore <u>outcome</u>.
- To make an enemy for <u>life</u>.

OMNIFY:

Stereophonic tones chanted by Buddhists.

OMNIPHOBIA:

A specific fear of the unspecified of nature.

OMNIPARITY:

Buddhist agreement.

OBLIVION:

- Cold storage of hope.
- Death of ambition.
- Graveyard of fame, and fortune.
- The big sleep-in. Restfulness without an annoying alarm.

OXYGONE:

That sharp realisation of becoming <u>breathless</u>.

OFF-OF:

Tautology.

OUTRAGE:

A pimple.

OLYMPIAN:

- Aged hobgoblin.
- Racy troublemaker.

ONCE:

That's quite enough!

OPPORTUNITY:

What <u>disappointment</u> follows.

OPPOSE:

The art of obstruction through <u>opposition</u>.

OPPOSITION:

Strategic manoeuvre in readiness to <u>oppose</u>.

OPTIMISM:

Successful certainty after an <u>opposition</u> to <u>oppose</u>.

OPTIMINIST:

Failed advantage to instil an <u>optimising</u> in <u>opposition</u> to <u>oppose</u>.

OXYMORON:

- Uneducated bovine. Under-skilled, and reliant on Social Welfare benefits.

- To the contrary:

- The *silence* is *deafening*.

- Only *one original*.

- It is *awfully good*.

- A night out with the *living dead*.

- Here's an *instant classic*.

- *Seriously funny* comedian.

- *Virgin birth*.

- *Christian Science*.

- *Christian bookstore*.

- *Endless infinity*.

- A *little giant*.

- *Religious education.*

- Done *accidentally* on *purpose.*

P:

P:

• Small green digestible seed often used as a play toy during meal times. Being flicked across a table at an opponent. Often as a <u>war</u> game of children and other playful creatures.

• Expressed laziness in wishing to micturate.

• (Symbolic) associated with persecution, preservation, foresight, intellect, curiosity, ego.

PHILOSOPHERS STONE:

The life resolves of a student of Stoicism. The courage to live well. To live your best life. Philosophy is the pillar. A fundamental of Stoicism, being a love of knowledge, and wisdom. The Stone: courage to wrestle with how to live your best life despite circumstance, or potential hindrance. The resolve to strive for excellence. Even as your life might feel as if it resembles the Greek mythic tale of Sisyphus; who was condemned to continually struggle with efforts to roll a bolder up a hill. Only to never reach the peak, for the bolder rolled back down at the closing of each day's efforts. Chinese philosopher, Sun Tzu wrote his philosophy of combat in "The Art of War". As a Stoic, or as someone striving to remain stoical in all life matters, how will your 'Art of war' manuscript read?

PIEBALD:

Pastry, lacking substance, or a filling.

PING PONG:

- A <u>noise</u>.
- High pitched, trumpeting reverberation of a fart.

PUNISH:

Not the discipline type. Rather, to pun paronomasia. To be silly with words and their meanings.

PACIFIER:

Oh, just suck it up.

PALMISTRY:

Employment of a doll bludger.

PESTICIDE:

Euphemism: describing the effects of an insects ass being the last thing on its mind at slamming into a windscreen, or other glass barrier.

PATHETIC:

Undoubted, the most forlorn of words ever conceived.

PREACH:

Type of religious fruit.

PHAROAH:

Trans daddy.

PALOODLES: (neo)

Man's best friends.

PAINTING:

The result of knocking that region around the elbow. Irreverently, the 'funny' bone.

PACIFIC:

- According to many, an ocean.
- The large even tempered body of water separating land masses.

PAST:

Gone.

PHEROMONE:

A (1992) movie: "Scent of a woman." Starring Al Pacino.

PILGRIM

PASTIME:

Long gone.

PAEDIATRICIAN:

A medical professional specialising in children, and other diseases.

PROHIBITION:

A diabolic engagement in lawmaking where the <u>bureaucracy</u>, and <u>republican</u> classes stifle, smother, and cause an abortion of innovation. Esp., those that a society has come to enjoy. Having been birthed to directly benefit a committee of self-aggrandising, self-proclaimed <u>puritans</u>.

PAGAN:

- (Lat) pagani, - the 'heathen rural folk'. Beliefs and rituals, and practices that predate christianity by centuries; including salvation by dying deity, physical resurrection, virgin birth, consuming deity body as purifying ritual, purgatory, baptism, worship of both good, and bad immortal entities, sacrifice, entreaty rituals.

- Anyone, or anything, or practice that is not approved, lauded acceptable by the puritan.

- The original reverence of what was considered unexplainable, or possessed material power.

- Genesis to religion.

PAIN:

Annoying, upsetting unpleasantness.

PAINFUL:

So much more annoying, upsetting, unpleasantness than <u>pain</u>.

PAINLESS:

Somewhere between <u>pain</u>, and <u>painless</u>.

PAINT:

No <u>pain</u>, <u>painful</u>, or <u>painless</u>.

PILGRIM:

- Risks associated with illegal drugs.

- A disenchanted <u>puritan</u> unable to convince outsiders of their personification of god according to their own conscious.

PAIRS/PEARS:

- United in opposition: day, and night; girl, and boy, light, and dark, moon, and sun, <u>life</u>, and <u>death</u>.

- Edible fruit stored on the <u>ark</u> for sustenance.

PRODITOMANIA:

"Aargh, you are all traitors."

PARTRIDGE:

Half sloped hilltop.

PEACOCK:

Contemptible edible green seed.

PIMLIMSEST:

The scar of a deceased <u>outrage</u>.

PLEASE:

An invocation to build a superstructure for levying.

PLEBICITE:

(Political) a vote to confirm the coronation of a Prime Minister, President.

PARALEGAL:

Differently abled legal practitioner.

PARSIMONIOUS:

Type of superior fruit.

PATERNALIST:

Fabric pattern designer.

PATHOLOGICAL:

Combined rationality.

PERDITION:

Hellish detention.

POLYPHONIC:

Operatic parrot.

PORTMANTEAU: (port-man-toe)

This woke-less wordbook.

PREREGRET:

That feeling immediately prior to a disappointment.

PRESTIDIGITATION:

Admirable swift typist.

PASSPORT:

- When a <u>warship</u>, <u>friendship</u>, <u>mateship</u>, <u>relationship</u> bungle their berthing at their appointed anchorage.

- A document used to ensure that an otherwise alienist is pointedly really an attractive reprobate, despite any <u>outrage</u>.

PRAMDICLE:

Frozen stroller.

PARLIAMENT (1):

A complex where a <u>quorum</u> of <u>elp</u> are given sanctuary in fulfilment of the minority rule over debatable presumption. Where a rostrum becomes the standard tool for when long-winded, noisome, bothersome rhetoric is exercised as a right of passage with impunity.

PARLIAMENT (2 - LONG: OE):

Thirteen year reign of power. Convened in 1640, and disbanded in 1653.

PARTICLE:

Part-time apostle.

PHARMACY:

Drug store for livestock, and hobby agronomists.

PLENTIFUL:

Bloated!

PEACE:

Slither of a spherical green seed called a vegetable.

PARAPET:

- Differently abled domestic companion.
- Airborne unit of highly trained combat animals.

PREAMBLE:

Exercise of stretching, prior to a leisurely stroll.

PREAMBULATE:

Before movement.

PESSIMISM:

The philosophy thrust on an <u>optimist</u> for the enjoyment of watching them squirm.

PROGRESSIVE:

Steady increase of aggression of speech, and act.

PHEONIX:

Original finger lickin' chook. Taught ancestors the value, convenience, and dangers of barbecued take-away foods. Known to the ancients as the first graduate an Honours Degree in <u>cryptozoology</u> for proving the debated theory surrounding <u>cryptograms</u>.

PHILOSOPHY:

• Interesting field of study that begins nowhere, in pursuit of nothing.

• British philosopher Ludwig Wittgenstein (1889 - 1951) once wrote an inspiring statement: "the limits of language are the limits of my world."

PHONOGRAPH:

A toy. The main goal of its use is life-giving; by forcing irritating <u>noises</u> from the inanimate.

PHONETIC: (Auth orig neo)

A disease of the unconscious to be uncontrollably urged to persistently 'check' a mobile devise for messages.

PUZZOMFUL: (neo)

Toxic, harmful, poisonous.

PRESENT:

- Make good use of it while you still can!
- See <u>today</u>, <u>now</u>.

PURITAN:

The fear exhibited that someone, somewhere, might be suffering dreadful happiness.

PARASITE:

- What is a parasite? A virus, bacteria, or other tiny infective agent. Often harmful, or corruptive of its host.

- What is the most resistant, corrosive parasite known? An idea! Ideas are the most infective, often corrosive of all parasites encountered by humanity. Whether well intentioned, or disruptive, ideas are most resilient. Once such a parasite takes hold in the conscious it breeds, ages, and matures. A parasitic idea is highly contagious. Acting in similar fashion to a "Chinese whisper" - spreading widely, becoming inflexible, and embellished the longer it remains able to multiply. E.g., the propaganda spread by Cromwell against Anne Boleyn (2nd wife to King Henry VIII -16c) who was beheaded following rumours of infidelity and other mistruths.

POLITICAL CORRECTNESS:

Abbr. (PC) is the term describing beliefs that all languages, beliefs, thoughts, actions must on all accounts be designed to be inoffensive to a potential opponent. Regardless, of logic, reason, empirical fact which are jettisoned for an ideological stance. To refuse political correctness is to suffer a barrage of incontestable, pestilential, and invidious assumption. Political correctness seeks to disengage, dehumanise, delegitimise, rewrite, reinvent, and deny reality, history, biology, science, and human ingenuity.

PERFECTION:

An illusion we all suffer. Accompanied by another delusional state - excellence. Which is only granted by the requests of a critic.

PHEMOMENOLOGY:

In possession of an astounding consciousness of self, and surroundings.

PENITENT:

When undergoing the wait of payback.

PIETY:

Obeisance offered to a supreme entity who pretended to wear the cloak of humanity.

PRIMORDIAL:

First sweetened drink invented.

PROCRUSTEAN:

To insist cutting off the outer layer of sandwiches.

PROPAGATE:

Purpose built barrier.

Q:

Q: (cue)

- Electrical charge.

- Jacksie with a tail.

- What the British are adept at without much complaint.

- Signals a beginning.

- Used in a game played on a table. The slotting of designated colour sphere's into an allotted pocket. Winner receives adulation, beer upon clearing their sphere's in a faster time than an opponent. Unless, a <u>barrage</u> ensues against someone believed to have cheated.

QUIXOTISM:

Extremely idealistic colloquialism.

QUARREL MAKER: (OWT)

Intentional dissenter; thrower of arrows in the form of barbed argument.

QUIXOTRY:

Irrational attempt at blasphemy.

QUORUM:

A determinative body of a select few. Chosen to safeguard a jaundiced opinion. Resulting in disadvantaging by demand the majority. The most well understood collective quorum is a <u>parliament</u>.

QUILL:

- Originally a writing instrument made from a feather nib dipped in ink. Now is obsolete. Has been replaced with a more durable, self-fulfilling, long-lasting model; both width, size, and able to hold various different colours. Is popular plastic model. Either are still considered by a featherhead as a most torturous device.

- Quill - the tongue of the mind.

R:

R: (ahr)

RADIENT:

- Incandescent insect.
- Euphorically industrious.

RIBALD:

Indulging in randy, liquorish behaviour.

RAWGABBIT:

- Naked elderly rabbit.

- Skinned rarebit being dressed, and prepared to recline properly at the table.

RAREBIT:

- According to some speech therapists, this animal could represent the extinct, Welsh, sociable plant-consuming mammal; who, despite having long ears, great eyesight, and being built to bound about swiftly when startled. It was forced into obscurity due to extensive 'spot-lighting', and other easter hunting games.

- Limited, odd, isolated sporadic bit.

RATIONAL:

Portioned delusion. Ignoring those ideologically encountered through observation, demonisation, and practical empirical knowledge.

RADISH:

Impressive, excellent food container.

RADICALISM:

A sadistic thought, and desire of modernism. That modern traditions be thrust upon the past lives, thoughts, desires, morals, ethical standards well into a future state.

RESIDUES:

Rent notification.

ROME (fall of):

The consequences of the decades of a moral, and ethical, and functional decline throughout ancient Rome was its complete demolition in history. The modern world has not learnt the lessons that ancient Rome has to teach. The moral, ethical, economic disarray witnessed in our day will again prove the decline, and demolition of all modern societies. Politician's, media, and other assumed 'elites' is blind to the fact they are contributing to an implosion, and dissolving of modern society. Western societies are decaying from the inside, and is on the verge of extinction. Not by a 'climatic' disaster, or other trumped up nonsense, but through an imbalance; of wealth, ethical, and moral aptitude.

REPRESENT:

Regifting an undesired present.

REFERENDUM:

A plea made by a medical professional when patient lists have become unserviceable.

RECIPLAY:

Playing with food.

R- (three):

- Formerly represented the purview of local Council: Rates, Roads, Rubbish.

- (Modern) represents: Radicalism (racism), Reparations, Revolution.

REVELATION:

A religious book of a <u>church</u> that should still be considered bumpkin.

RETRIBULATION:

The reemergence of trials, vengeance, and other punishments inflicted upon any who dare have a misguided notion to open, and read the <u>revelation</u>.

RELATIONSHIP:

A vessel of many amicable alliances.

REMONTANT:

Fertile insect.

REVOLUTION:

An event that takes place every time any distance is travelled on a road toward the alteration of futility.

REAL

RELIGION:

The practice of emptying the mind, becoming void of character, while forsaking reality. Reliant on confused reason at asking those caught by its vacuum to reconsider a believed, but proven falsehood. Read in the dusty old necrological writings of illiterates. Claiming to have supported a fanciful personality.

RESEMBLANCE:

Counterfeit original.

REMITTANCE:

(Boxing) the devastating blows traded by combatants.

REALISM:

An art of depicting, or inflicting upon a society the actual, or imagined panoramic perspective of the world.

RELATIVE:

Neighbour.

REAL:

Transparent.

RIGHTANIUM: (Auth orig neo)

Modern life force that urges acts, and speech pleasing to another. The consequences: a chemical imbalance or arhwrongnium.

REALITY:

• The nightmare of 'love island' and other programming of nonsense.

- Differs to 'news' broadcasts, and fear-porn from activists.

- Is outside, tangible, observable, engaging, and able to be destroyed through sensitivity.

- The vacuum of Space.

- Written on the face.

REPUBLIC:

Where authority, and public responsibility is transferred to one narcissistic authoritarian. Who only exists by optional obedience to public opinion.

QUESTION: what is the difference between <u>reality</u>, and fiction?
ANSWER: fiction must be appreciably sensible.

REDUNDANT:

Superfluous, disposable insects past their prime.

ROUE: (ro-ay)

A naughty elderly geezer.

RIOT:

A popular mode of disturbance, and mass activity of disruption of the innocent bystander by a rebel.

R.I.P.:

Popular headstone epitaph engraving. Erroneously meaning Rest In Peace. But, should be understood to mean; *Reduced In Pizzazz.*

REASON:

- Weighed chances.
- Precursor to prejudice.

REBEL:

Progeny to radicalism.

RECONCILIATION:

Brief cessation of hostilities to <u>reconsider</u> the dead.

ROPE:

Tightly woven fibrous <u>cacti</u> once worn as an unfashionable garment as a statement to heed for a certain demographic. Used to remind the maladjusted, and very naughty of society of our feebleness, and morality. Not so fashionable nowadays. Although still quite prominent in some regions as a <u>life</u>-less example to the presumed, indicated belligerent.

ROAD:

An appointed bitumen strip allowing for smoother, faster, less treacherous deviations. In a safer transition from one futility, to another more, or less scenic futility.

RECONSIDER:

To enact, validate, sanction, impose, and legalise a decision previously agreed.

S:

SOCIAL DEMOCRACY:

• Oxymoron.

• Democracy is a freedom to choose how to be governed. The population chooses its representative governing body. Socialism, is when a government determines social, productive, economic lifestyles.

• A highly regulated population of virtue signallers.

SABOTAGE:

• Era of the clog. From *sabot* - kind of wooden shoe, + age.
• A box of cards - see *sabot*.
• Age of deliberate acts of inconvenience.

SADDEN:

The lair, hide out, secreted place where the downtrodden voice grievances.

SKRANKY:

Bones near showing, skins leathery, and saggy.

SARDONIC:

A genuinely sour cynic.

SCIENCE:

- The art of dropping little things upon other things to review potential reactions.

- Systematic study of structural, and physical behaviour for the purpose of testing, hypothesising, and adopting, or discarding previous knowledge.

SHADENFREUDE:

- Mocking of another's misfortune.
- (Modern) a prick, bastard...

SUNDAY:

Not the day of rest. But, the day after this day before.

SATURDAY:

According to Jewish tradition, the day of rest.

SCHOOL:

An institution called upon by parents where semiliterates babysit their illiterate offspring. Specifically, while the parent busies themselves with other interests; work, play, or other activity. The children sent to such an institute, are hoped to pick up a sense of literacy so decent conversations could be had around the meal table.

SILLYGISM:

Reasoning that is invalid. May contain a grain of sensibility, and <u>truth</u>. Much like this dictionary.

SATAN:

- A creative misstep of a deity.

- Was formerly kicked in the butt, stumbled headlong, and fell from the great lighthouse of the heaven. According to some, is most terrifying to behold, or align with. Being <u>now</u> a farouche Mephistophelian, sporting very mean, sulphurous intent. Yet, still cruises about the earth realms in a <u>warship</u> seeking long lost <u>friendship</u>, and/ or <u>mateship</u> restored. All manners of human vice, as with countless statutes of <u>puritan</u> courtship are placed on his shoulders. Allowing for a belief in this life that all hardships are as a direct result, and fault attributed to him. Satan made me write this!

SNUFF: (neo)

To take offence.

SALTANT:

- Sovereign insect to Arabic states.

- Insect employee to saliferous products manufacturing at the 'Pillar of Salt' factory of the Dead Sea regions.

SCOWL:

Pissed off owl, or nocturnal bovine.

SEVERAL:

To dismember everything.

SOPHOCLES:

"A man's affairs become diseased when he wishes to cure evils, with evils."

SUPERNATURAL:

Greatest, unprocessed organic products.

SOUTH:

- Opposing <u>north</u>.
- 90degree lower than <u>west</u>, or <u>east</u>.

SEGUE:

A <u>road</u>.

SOMEWHEN:

Who knows?

SAINT:

Succeeding death. Is an upgrade to First class sinner. One who is recognised as having been not so dull as other pedestrians.

SPEL:

Mystical oracle, speech, or hidden knowledge.

SLAVE:

Slavery visits they who do not know how to survive on <u>alittle</u>.

SYLLABUS:

Party transportation.

SIN/SYN:

- A delusional state of self-flagellation.

- Whatever performance, attitude, opinion that differs to that of the <u>puritan</u>.

- Hubris of the clergy, and other religious authorities.

SLANG:

The whiplash, voyeur, and vagabond of language.

SINBAD:

Apparently!

SINAI:

Transgressing automaton, droid, machine, bot; <u>A.I.</u>.

SHAMPOO:

Cheap imitation excrement.

SELF-ESTEEM:

"I think I can, I think I can." Puffed Thomas the Tank Engine.

SNOB:

Anyone who thinks their speech, or action is more betterer, more properer than another's. A virtue signaller.

STARVING SHARK:

Phrase expressing one's inability at showing compassion. Someone acting as a starving shark, attacks an opposition with unruly sentiment.

T:

T: (tee)

Is for turnip, and other troubling protuberant vegetables.

TANGENT:

Dark complexion gentleman.

TURKEY BACON:

- Hired security.
- Imitation <u>geep</u>.

TOADSTOOL:

- Amphibian excrement.
- Amphibious stepladder.

TRIFECTA:

To be inflicted with three diseases simultaneously.

TRIANGLE:

- Sundial of the Ancient Egyptians.
- "If triangles had a god, it would have three sides."

TIME:

- An illusion.

- 'Time heals, but waits for no man.'

- Time heals only through <u>forgetfulness</u>.

- Is not linear. The best of times are had when we waste it.

- Is however one perceives it; when running late, or behind time, it's best to announce "Sorry I'm late, but my time is more precious than yours."

TODAY:

Is the same present moment for all of <u>life</u>. Whether long, short the <u>present</u>, today, converges on the same point.stretching behind, or into a future. Today, is the constant of life.

TWICE:

Yes, - again!

TOMORROW:

A future replicating of <u>now</u>.

TROGLODYTE:

Froggish dinosaur.

TRINITY:

Audience.

TELEPHONE:

- Device for annoying relatives.

- Play thing of toddlers.

- Device with a goal of bringing to an ear canal the wonder of a god-like experience/ encounter through ventriloquism.

TWITLER:

Anonymous social media user. Bullying others in to submission, or admission of a perceived guilt.

TRUTH:

- Is always laughed at, ridiculed, dismissed as falsehood only to be later accepted.

- Is always verifiable, accurate, loyal, legitimate, and not easily tarnished.

TREE:

Jocular trinity.

TORTOISE:

- Not a hare.
- The disparity mode of a gofer/ golf buggy.
- Speed differential of mechanical equipment.

TRANSLUNARY:

Another side to behaviour influences of <u>amun</u>.

TOWNSHIP:

Collective: <u>warship</u>, <u>mateship</u>, <u>relationship</u>, and other ships appropriately berthed. After forsaking their usual inclination to purposefully <u>passport</u>, and remain singular in purpose.

TRUCKULANT:

Aggressive heavy haulage.

THEORY OF EVERYTHING:

First, at a <u>time</u> and place vastly distant to the here and <u>now</u>, there was nothing. Nothing was not void; however, but was pregnant with potential. So pregnant was nothing that it could no longer contain it. Something was soon birthed, having exploded outward, something bubbled, burped, boiled. Eventually, congealing into an organised mass which soon changed its name to matter; with monikers, substance, or other stuff.

Hidden within this other stuff was in essence called <u>life</u>. Life eventually became known as sentients. Becoming animals of all varieties, and intelligence. The best of sentients became known as humankind, for they did find there were no others capable in skill, prowess. Naturally, humankind did think itself above all others, proving its many skillsets like becoming great <u>bergmasters</u>, and other types of maestro. With such a high praise of itself, humankinds have a much <u>difficult time</u> to truly harmonise with <u>allot</u> of other stuff. Including differently <u>abled</u> humankinds. To great relief of much matter that followed, humans have also proven to fall into a comatose state after several decades. Becoming like any other matter, inanimate. This seems to occur on average, sometime after 42! Human interaction begins to wane, eventually stopping for a great rest. After-which, matter resumes control with much celebration. In harmony matter consumes the inanimate humankind.

TALK:

An impulse of little, or no purpose.

U:

U: (ew)

I am not U. Neither can U be I, or other IU. So, none should be indicted as the source, or cause of U presenting with an adverse reaction of some unknown offense. U, however is a noun, not a pronoun. Granted, U is likely a fashioned Upperclass plurality. So, U does possess a potential sinister demeanour. Presenting as socially exclusive. U, might therefore fit comfortably with a modern socially senseless, applauded pretence.

U-BOAT:

Floating on <u>aback</u>.

UNSAVOURY:

An unredeemable sinner.

UNSEX:

To change <u>agenda</u>. To make other than an original.

UNSOULCLOGGED:

- Free spirited.
- <u>Breathless</u>.

UNFORTUNATE:

Not wealthy.

UGLYOGRAPHY:

To spel, or right rongly. Putting commas, everywhere except; where they, are , not required or, should be placed let alone , isolated. And to use and, to begin, a sentence. Also, don't never use a double negative or leave a sentence ending without a full stop

UGSOME:

Somewhat repulsive.

UMBRA:

Parasol of a Galactic body.

UXORIOUSNESS:

The dilemma at realising affections have stayed with your wife.

UFOLOGIST:

- Not an alienist.
- Follower in the latest trends.
- Unworldly ufo.

U.F.O.:

- Not an E.T.V., Extraterrestrial vehicle.
- *U*ngainly *F*atidic *O*bamulation (graceless prophetic wanderer).

UNITARIANISM:

3 to 1: what are the odds?

URBANITY:

The insanity of city life.

UNCTION:

To exclude 'a' from performance influence.

UTOPIA:

- Illusory perfectionism.

- From Greek: 'ou', no + 'topos', place. Meaning no place. Factually, is a void. Is nullity, nothing. Related to humanity, humans become void of being.

- Is one of the adversary lessons of Socialism 101.

- According to socialism, is achieved by diminishing the world populations to 500million persons, so to 'balance nature'.

UNIQUE:

Totally not like anything, or common. Uniques however is no more unique a word than any other. Yet, unique is stated to possess a distinction; an eccentric individualism.

UBIQUITOUS:

The deranged, bumptous tentacles of twenty first century wokeness.

UNBRIDLED:

To beat a hasty retreat from a groom at the alter.

UNIVERSITY:

• More expensive institute than a <u>school</u>. Yet, surprisingly has similar outcomes, and goals for students.

• The institute employed to churn from the meat grinder copious maladjusted, insecure automatons bent on the destruction of previous standards, and mores with ideas claimed to be of 'higher learning'. More principled, ethical, and of greater benefit. The archetype of all other ideologies.

• A place where reasonably literate, but ill-informed persons attend to learn how to become a collective.

• The collective that espouses that modernity be overturned through a separatism.

• Where solace is found with like-minded pathetic creatures bent on the abolishment of modernity.

UNDERCLUB:

An underdeveloped <u>clubbable</u>.

URCHIN: (OWT)

Child.

UNITED NATIONS:

• A highly suspicious organisation formed after World War II. Run entirely by an elitist class of wealthy autocrats. Its goal: is to bark as loudly as possible, frighten as many people as possible with ever increased menacing rhetoric on a variety of politically charged topics. To manipulate, and bully the world into compliance, acceptance, and agreement of its desires.

• Originally, formed to procure safety of world populations through a promotion of world peace, security, and cooperation of world Nations.

• Modern: is a conglomerate of barking, wailing whiners, whinges determined to Bogart world populations onto paths that secure for the elites that individual, national sovereignty is controlled, undermined.

V:

V: (vee)

VACUOUS:

An unresponsive vacuum.

VAMPISH:

Somewhat bloody sucker.

VAPID:

In an alphabetical sense: is much speedier than rapid.

VAUNTED:

A disturbing taunting dream-state of a <u>vampish</u>.

VERNACULAR:

Matriarch of a vampish.

VALOUR:

Gambler's hope.

VERMINT:

Entomophagous foodstuffs laced with an aromatic culinary plant extract to enhance palatability.

VANITY:

- Mirror.

- The contribution of a blockhead to world GDP, to the nearest worth in ass.

VIRTUE:

A variety of teetotalism.

VANGUARD:

Security dog.

VOTE:

A symbolic gesture of power handed to a muttonhead ensuring the ruination of a State, and/or country.

V-NECK:

Odd neckline.

V-AERIAL:

Rarebit ears.

VEGAN(ism):

Someone believing that abetter sustainability of the Earth, and its resources is gained by ending the world war between carnivorous, and ovolactarian citizens. Specifically, that all carnivores renounce their diabolical murderous insensitivities. To transition to an ovolactarian, entomophagous lifestyle.

VULPACTUATED: (obs. 1671)

Red riding-hood's nemesis.

VALENTINE'S DAY:

A christianised mating ritual of the ancient Roman festival - Lupercalia. Where fertile couples exchange, or extend propositions, and pleasantries to each other in hopes of coupling; even if the result is "friends with benefits."

VANISHING DAY:

Resurrection.

W:

W: (double ew)

WANTON:

Asian type fortune cookie.

WASPISH:

Just like an irritated, middle-upperclass protestant.

WEHRD: (word - Auth orig neo)

- Alt. Spelling. Phonetic sound of word.
- When released into the open, wehrds cannot be retracted.

WASTEFUL:

Large of girth.

WARSHIP:

Vessel with hostile intent.

WEREWOLF:

A carnivore suffering the haemorrhaging effect of a persistent-loss to intellectual function.

WAILBONE:

Aching ribs.

WOKE:

- Broke.
- Insignificant abusive huckster.
- Less abrasive term for <u>puritan</u>.

WEST:

- Opposing <u>east</u>.
- Neither <u>north</u>, or <u>south</u>.

WHITE:

Much lighter, and dazzling than black.

WASTEFUL

WAR:

What is it good for?

- Profit.

- Power.

- The 0.01% controlling the wealth, energy sources, life situations of the 99.9%.

- Prevents the evolution of the Human species.

- Keeps a foothold on the status quo; the majority in subservience to the minority.

- Is a political game of chess between Nations, their rulers. Against another. Is played with live chess pieces with little regard to how the chess piece might feel about being fodder.

- Is an often orchestrated reality. War does not just happen. Each are strategically structured, and orchestrated by profiteers.

WORK:

A menial accomplishment performed in leu of another task acted out this is more pleasurable.

WORKER:

The lever of ineptopcracy. Those who have resigned to slavery of Procrustean tasks in exchange for a subsistent lifestyle.

X:

X: (ex)

Former partner who requires alimony, but no other supports.

X-RAY:

- Lightless.

- Does not succumb to conditional harassment, or the embarrassment of exposure.

XEROX:

To multiply, or deny the breeding of oxen.

XANTHIPPE:

Ill-tempered, and scornful.

XENOTRANSPLANTATION:

- Transhumanism.
- The transfer of non-human materials into a human host.

XENODOCIUM:

Fancy word of a superior person meaning hotel.

Y:

Y: (why)

Standard question for inquiry.

YEAR:

A period of being subjected to 365 disappointments.

YESTERDAY:

A period of time that happened before now.

YODEL:

Yoda's wife.

YAUCHILE: (OE)

To walk awkwardly, and with difficulty.

YAWMAGORP: (1887)

A layabout reclining on a lounge.

YO:

- One half of a sweet biscuit.
- Australian colloquial greeting, "Yo! Bro, how goes it?"
- An oscillating toy of string that always sways one way.

Z:

Z:

Denotes sleep.

ZAP:

Brings, or destroys life essence.

ZAPHOD BEEBLEBOX:

(Hitchhiker's Guide to the Galaxy)

- Bicephalous.

- Tri-armed 'president' of the Universe.

- Is self-absorbed.

- Hedonistic.

- Irresponsible.

- Clever.

- Untrustworthy.

- Imaginative.

- Insinuative.

- Extroverted.

- Prone to tantrums.

- Voted the 'worst' dressed sentient being of the Universe.

- Exists as much as any other fantastic demiurge.

- Stole the 'Improbability Drive Galactic Starship' after winning the Universal Presidential Elections he was supposed to loose dramatically.

Zaphod is then well suited to pursue Universal fame as a god-like being.

ZEAL:

Unchecked passion of those born <u>yesterday</u>. Occurring at a time not too distant preceding the disease 'apathy of indifference.'

ZIG-ZAG:

- An ambulation test during a night out.
- The predetermined resolve of a predestrian zig-zag class. The <u>bumptous</u>.

ZEBRA:

Support device for the remarkably buxom.

AFTERWEHRD:

Here then is an **afterwehrd**. No others follow!

BIBLIOGRAPHY:

BARRETT. G. The Official Dictionary of Unofficial English. Copyright©2006 by McGraw-Hill Companies, Inc. Kobo Digital edition.

BRISTOW. J. Old English Words and Terms. Copyright© Joy Bristow, 2001. Digital edition. Published 2012. Kobo digital edition.

CONLEY.C. One Letter Words: A Dictionary. Copyright© Craig Conley 2005 HarperCollins Publisher's. E-book.

DENT. S. An Emotional Dictionary. Copyright© Susie Dent, 2022. John Murray (Publishers). Kobo ed.

EDWARDS. E. Words, Facts, and Phrases: A Dictionary of curious, quaint, and out-of-the-way matters. Barnes, and Nobel. Copyright© 2011. Kobo ed.

MACCABE. C., and YANACEK. H. (Editors) Key Words for Today: A 21st Century Vocabulary. (The Key Words Project) Copyright© Oxford University Press, 2018. Kindle ed.

WATERS. C. A Dictionary of Old Trades, Titles, Occupations. Text Copyright© Colin Waters, 1999, 2002. Digital Edition distributed in 2014 by Bookmasters, Inc.

Don't miss out!

Visit the website below and you can sign up to receive emails whenever Steve Morgan publishes a new book. There's no charge and no obligation.

https://books2read.com/r/B-A-TAKAB-OOJOC

BOOKS 2 READ

Connecting independent readers to independent writers.

Did you love *Wokeless Dictionary (A Wicked Wordbook)*? Then you should read *DECONSTRUCTING ENDTIME DELUSIONS (A STUDY OF CHRISTIAN ENDTIMES)*[1] by Steve Morgan!

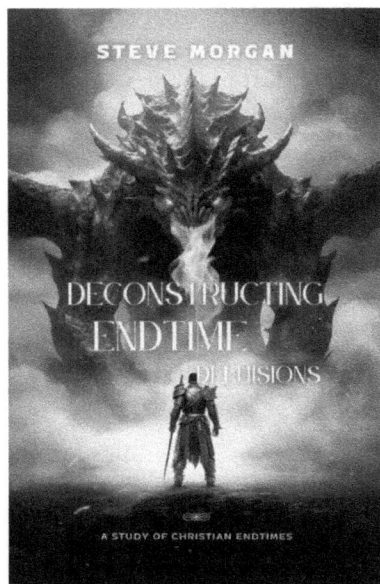

What do you think about the End Times? Is it a valid religious prospect; a prolepsis that sets your world atwitter? If you are someone open to different ways of viewing christian credenda; if you are open to perspectives that are unlikely taught by a believing institution; if you are curious about why humans believe, observe, and guess certain favoured end time practices; if you have ever wondered from where, or just how true certain beliefs are, then welcome aboard. Strap yourself in for an unconventional journey through several end time topics. This book is a collated compendium of the author's Ten year personal study efforts into numerous Christian End time proposals. Fed up with what

---

1. https://books2read.com/u/bxBolD

2. https://books2read.com/u/bxBolD

seemed the brainwashing of nonsense the author began in 2010 to scribble thoughts and study conclusions about the religiously, christian concept of end time. This is an investigation into probing questions for why the believing community is so resolute regarding certain aniconic ecclesiastical teachings. Such as Rapture, Antichrist, Angels, Demons, Nephilim of Genesis chapter six & a variety of other topics. The continuing years spent in research, and writing meant that this investigation actively expanded the further practical, lucid answers were sought to the countless questions that study interests raised.

Many conclusions surprised this author, and so are likely to gob-smack an audience also. It is not technically a monograph of what a reader might assume as a conventional study of the christian religion, or various end-time presumptions. Rather, this study is an unconventional, enlightening peering into some enigmatic End Time Apocalyptic topics. Told through the eyes, and with a curiosity of a former believer. Welcome to the Revelation!

About the Author

Born into a Christian family, in 1971, Steve applied himself to an extensive study of Christianity through the 1990's. Leading to a departure from the faith in the mid 2000's. In 2012 Steve was forced into retirement with a disability. Since, his life has grown with several interests emerging. An amateur parrot breeder, amateur Colour Pencil artist, writer, reader & avid lawn Bowler. Is a fan of quality film, documentaries, & intelligent comedy: "Fluffy", & Bill Bailey. He has an ever widening assortment of interests; Current affairs, quirky history, Stoicism, philosophy, & Egyptian History. Never married, he lives alone in regional Victoria, Australia, with his beloved parrots. Interest in paronomasia, & neologisms began in earnest during the worlds longest lockdown in Victoria, Australia during the recent Covid-19 pandemic, 2021. Producing The Standard Religiously Irrelevant Version, a parodied edition of several Christian folklore.